COCAINENOMICS

FROM COCA TO WALL STREET

Cocainenomics by DaVaughn Kidd
Copyright © 2019 by DaVaughn Kidd

ISBN: 9781794570092

DEDICATION

I dedicate this book to Latoya V Kidd my loving sister who has been a great inspiration to me and the encouraging whisper in my ear.

ACKNOWLEDGEMENTS

I am and will be forever grateful to God for changing my life! He has giving me the gift to teach others how to maximize their wealth potential through biblical financial principles. I have found his benevolence!

FOREWORD

Reading DaVaughn's work, I'm not surprised that I was taken with his exploration of how the Street economy mimics Wall Street. This book managed to be a potent mix of Urban economics with a sophistication that reaks of every day life and entertainment, because what comes through again and again in DaVaughn's writing is his recognition of the power of fictional worlds with the twist of everyday economics we have all seen or have witnessed or have had to cope with in the real world in which we all live.

I hope DaVaughn will forgive the suggestion that the most poignant creation in these pages was one he began writing at the impressively young age of twenty. The young mastermind title character creates imagined world of criminal behavior to cope with his circumstances, says much about the uses of fiction by all of us—and, perhaps, about its dangers as well, as beneath DaVaughn's seemingly cold heart, wealth is not just created.

The weight of consequences: the tragic results of "harmless" street dealing the Urban neighborhood raw admonition and greed it is bone-chilling. "The Most Terrifying story of Betrayal ever Written"

BGF

TABLE OF CONTENTS

1. The Beginning.   9

2. Mexico   13

3. The Call   17

4. Our Pact.   25

5. Time To Roll!   31

6. What I'm Going To Be   37

7. Banished.   45

8. Family Is Everything!   61

9. Wish I Was Innocent Again   67

10. Only If You Are a Cartel Member!   79

11. The Reign of Terror.   93

12. Protecting Your Families Future   105

13. Live By The Code, Die By The Code   121

14. The Conclusion and Heart of The Matter   139

Chapter 1
THE BEGINNING

I started out in life as a regular boy. Nothing was really no different in my house, then any other house on the street. My Mom was a Security Bank Programmer and my Dad owned his own business. I had one brother and two sisters that I loved very dearly and life was great! My dad would take us to New York every summer, so he could give us a lecture on being a minority and how we must learn to make money.

He would always say, "If you buy something of high value, you owe it to yourself to figure out how to get your money back from the corporation. Wall Street is a culture, not a place." Boy, was he right!

My brother, Cliff, was the biggest influence in my life. He was only six years older than me, but to me, it seemed like he knew everything! My dad was grooming Cliff to take over the family business. My father would say to Cliff, "You are next to take over this business after me. I hope you will do a good job of taking care of the family."

In our family, my father is the sun and the moon and what he says is to be followed and not questioned. Cliff would say, "Old traditions is what will take this family into the next phase of wealth. When I take over, things will change for the better. "My dad would say, "Sons, mimic their fathers, and I hope what you are saying is true."

The family business made life better for us. It gave the family a great start in life. The company was started by my father and his brothers, but they all had different ideas on how the company should be run. One brother believed that doing everything hands-on, was the way to run the company and the other brother went along with what he said.

Even though they may have disagreed at times, each brother had a "gift" to make money. Funny thing is, the banker of the company was my Grandmother! She ran the show when it came to them. She ruled them with an iron hand. She was a very pretty lady with light, red hair, brown honey skin and had an iron Will to match her beauty.

My Grandmother had a dream for each of them that would push them all into success. My Grandmothers' nickname was "Ginny girl" and was born in a small town outside Mexico City called Pokito Ciudad.

She would tell us stories of how beautiful her town was and how she missed her family there. She had migrated away from that small town trying to flee a political system that had become too corrupt to live in.

"One day," she would say, "I will return to my town and live with my family once again, but I cannot leave this country until I have either a job at home to keep me busy or I take my family away from there."

She would always share her story about how her and her sister were so poor, that they would go to the river close to the town and fetch water to sell to the men working construction. She would say, "In my country, men of power come in many forms. In the United States, political power runs the country, but in my country, he who has the money runs the show.

Here, you have money everywhere. There, money comes sparingly.

One day, I am going to apply to the Embassy there and see if I can get a job in Mexico City and guess what my little boy, you will be going with me.

Your father feels that you need a change in your life and what better change, than another country. I will make you stronger than your father and I will introduce you to the other half of your family.

You only know the American side, but oh my son, there is a whole, big family waiting for you. I have sent them pictures of all of you!"

Chapter 2
MEXICO

I have been in Mexico for one year now and to my surprise, I love this country!

I found myself wondering, "What does this place have to offer me?" On June 16, 1988, my grandmother and I awoke to a blistering summer heat. It had to be 80 degrees and it was only 8:00 am!

I started my daily routine of rinsing the milk bottles out and going to get the morning paper for my Grandmother when I heard the phone ring. It sounded as if, she was talking to her brother. At this particular time, I had never met any of her family. She would always tell me, "You will meet everyone when my brother gets out of prison."

In Mexico, you can go to jail for a list of things. If you have no job, prison camp is what you would get. "I haven't seen my brother in years. He is so dear to me," she said. I gave her a hug and said, "Then, he is dear to me too." I could see he meant a lot to her.

As we started our day, we got dressed and headed into town, Pokito Ciudad which means, little city. My Grandmother began to tell me that she had not been into the city since she was a little girl. I can remember asking her, "Are you scared?"

"Not scared my darling, but nervous I guess." I could see she was holding back something. The city, to me, seemed to be located in the middle of nowhere. It was like a city built in the middle of a desert. As we got closer to her part of the town, I could tell this was not like Mexico City, with the hustle and bustle.

Instead of lots of cars, there were donkeys. "Roll the window up, she said." "DaVaughn, this is poor; people in the States have it great, even the poor." She squeezed my hand and said,

"Now you will see what men of power look like. Here, man is not judged by what he has, but how he shares what he has been given."

The car arrived in front of this ranch. It looked like something out of an old, western movie. "Now, you be on your best behavior. Be very respectful and don't ask questions. Just keep quiet. Do you hear me?" "Yes," I answered.

We started up the driveway, when we were stopped by two groups of men. They started screaming something in Spanish, but I didn't understand what it was. My Grandmother started yelling back.

One of the men ran up to the house, I guess to make contact with the owners. When the man returned, he whispered something in the other man's ear.

He continued muttering something to the other men and then led the way to the main house. On the front porch was a plaque that read plomo or plata. "Grandmother, what does that say?" "You will know soon enough." I never forgot that sign!

Later when I got home, I looked up the phrase. It meant lead or silver. I was still duped, but I knew in Mexican life, one is offered, either gold or bullets. Hence the phrase, lead or silver.

Suddenly, the door flung open and this little man came running out of the house. He was crying as he ran up to us, and threw his arms around my Grandmother, lifting her off the ground. I had never seen my Grandmother so happy. She burst into tears! I walked up to the porch, sat down, and quietly waited. Then she said, "This young man here is my grandson. He belongs to my son, Michael. This one has our father's spirit in him, he will one day run the American family after his father with his brother. "Hello, he said witha strong Spanish accent, "do you know who I am?"

I am your great uncle. My name is Haffi and this is my son, the head of the family, Marcel, your uncle." My Grandmother gave him a big hug, kissed him on the cheek and said, "I thank you from the bottom of my heart for allowing me to come here.

I have missed this place for so long. I was afraid to contact the family, in fear that you would have ill feelings for me because I left." "Oh no, he said, your son gave us so much and you are the reason for our survival, not me.

It is I, who should thank you. I am the Patron now, and we shall speak, once you have had time to settle in." She smiled and kissed him again.

Excited, I asked if I could go look around. "Sure, this is your home. Just don't wonder to far." I went to the edge of the gate where I saw men walking around with dogs and what seemed to be fire arms. The weapons would twinkle and sparkle as the sun struck them. "Hombre, come with me," I heard from a voice behind me.

"I want to introduce you to the rest of the family." As we were walking, he asked, "So, how do you like Mexico? You are a long way from home. I know your father. He's a very nice man. He has done a lot for us. When you see him again, you remember that I have told you to thank him.

He will know what it means." He then called for Marcel Jr. and a little donkey kid came running over. "This is your cousin, your primo in Latin, you two are the same age. Take him around and show him the rancho." "Yes," Junior said,

bowing his head to his father. I have never seen such control. It seemed that Marcel Senior ran the whole show.

Junior reminded me of a military child. Everything was Yes Sir, No Sir. After Marcel Sr. left, I asked, "Does everyone speak English?" He said, "My father and I do. My grandfather can speak some. I want to learn to speak English well. Can you teach me while you are here and I will teach you Spanish? That's how me and Marcel met on a humble.

Chapter 3
THE CALL

Early one morning, I got a call from my father "I am coming to see you and I am bringing your brother with me." I got so happy, I almost peed in my pants. "When Poppa? When are you coming?" He stated, "We will be there tomorrow; do not tell your Grandmother, I want to surprise her." "Si, "I replied. Poppa said, "I see you are using Spanish more.

It's good you are using the language. It will one day be the second language in the United States. Now, I have to go pack my bags for the trip."

I could not wait to see my Poppa! I immediately called Marcel to tell him that my dad was coming to see me.

"Great, we can take them to the horse trails. What are we doing today? Are we coming out to the house?" I could hear the disappointment in his voice when I said, "No," so I made plans to go after I went to the market with my Grandmother. "I will have dad send the car for you." he said.

I arrived there around one o'clock in the evening. It was hot as usual. It seems as if the sun follows you here. It was too hot to ride the horses, so we just decided to go for a walk on the trails around the house. We started down this one trail that had these markings on the trees. "What do these markings mean, Marcel?" He said he didn't know, but I could tell he was lying. We got to the end of the trail and we heard a motor or something running.

We walked toward the sound. The trees were thick and all I could think is, I hope I don't get bit by a snake! Marcel seemed to know where we were going, so I just followed him through this mini forest. The path he took us on, lead us to this massive field were there were rows and rows of what looked like mini trees." What kind of plants are these Marcel?" He said, "My Poppa calls them Coca.

Whenever, I have seen it being harvested, it is used for the sap in the leaves and the rest is burned. I think it is like aspirin or something, because Poppa always refers to it as Narco. It looks like milk when it is drained from the leaves, but it smells like dung.

Whatever, it is for, Poppa makes a lot from it. It has to be important, because my Grandfather served time in jail for it." I never forgot what I saw that day.

I could not wait for my father and brother to arrive. Cliff was my father's oldest son.

He loved Cliff very much and he was grooming him to take over the business. But Cliff had a street mentality and would not accept the fact, that business is done with a hand shake, and not a gun. He would jokingly say to my father; "Oh, I shake their hand as my men reach for their guns." My father never found that joke funny.

Cliff loved me like a father loves his son. I can remember a time when he spotted me hanging out with some friends. It was in the winter of 1988. The snow was coming down like a thick blanket. He must have seen me from a distance. He pulled up in his car and rolled the window down and screamed. "Where is your hat and gloves?" I had forgotten them at home. "You will catch a cold. Here, take my hat. (It was his favorite hat.)

Put this on. I can get another hat, but I only have one little brother." In Cliffs' mind, he thought it was his duty to stay on top of me because our father did not have the time to do so. Poppa spent all his life wheeling and dealing. Cliff made it a point to share affection, like I was his kid, because Poppa had no time for it.

When Cliff and my dad arrived in Mexico, it was a big deal for me! On the ride from the airport, Cliff noticed that the police did not have guns.

I told him that Grandmother explained that the joke is, if you gave them guns, all they would do is use them on the people. The army has plenty, if needed. I was so excited, watching everyone and everything! My father had this look in his eye, like he was excited about something too. I figured it was because he was about to see his mother.

We arrived in front of the house and the taxi driver was trying to explain how much the fare was for the ride, but my Dad had no clue of what he was saying. My Dad spoke "no Spanish" at all. Seeing the opportunity to impress them both, I asked for my Dad's wallet and handed the man what he asked for.

It felt so good to be able to show my Dad that, I too, have talent, not just Cliff. In Mexico, you take Spanish twice a day in school. I have so much to show you guys." "The first thing I must do is see my mother," Dad said, and with that said, we headed upstairs.

My Grandmother had been cooking all day, because I had told her that Marcel was coming for dinner as not to ruin the surprise. She was sitting at the kitchen table when I called out to her to come see who is here to see you. "Who is it, Chico?" "It's a surprise." Dad peaked his head out and she let out a scream out that you would hear at a New Years' party!

She covered him with hugs and kisses. Then Cliff peaked his head out and she started crying! She was so happy to see them and it was good to see her so happy.

At dinner, she told my father that her brother was home and that he must go pay his respects. "Which one is home, Momma? You have so many siblings. She said, "Marcel's father."

And then it happened, my Dad's face tuned pale. It was like being at a party and the music stopped. I could see that this was not good news to him. My Grandmother said, "It is time for them to repay you for all you have done for them. Wait until you see the rancho. They have made it into a beautiful place." "Momma, do I have to go see them?" Her face became cold and she raised her voice in a tone I only heard, when she was upset. She said, "You cannot hide from your family and you cannot visit Mexico without paying respect and that's that."

Cliff asked, "Grandmother, what is your family like?" She said, "To make it short, if the Black man stuck together the way Mexicans do, then no Black man would go hungry. Family is everything here. There is a Patron in every family."

She explained how our father is the Patron over us and how the "Patron" runs every member of his family.

He gets paid for it too, plus all members have to live on the same land. "You mean to tell me the whole family lives in one place?" Cliff asked. "Yes, she said, it is 40 of us and everyone is a family member. You have to see it. It is very beautiful."

Cliff said, "Let me get this straight. One man runs the show and everyone has to listen to the head of the family, even the older members must take orders?" He seemed strangely excited. I asked if Cliff and I could be excused from the table.

I just had to ask my questions.

As we walked, I told Cliff about the statue of a golden angel that I wanted him to see. She was made of real gold. We got to the statue and sat on the steps. "Cliff, I have a question to ask you and don't think me stupid by this question, but what is coca?" Cliffs eyes became wide. "Why do you ask?"

"Because I have seen the plants, but I don't know what it is used for. What do you make with this plant? I heard it is used for the sap in the leaves, but you can't eat it.

Why is the sap important?" With this stupid chuckle, Cliff said, they use it to make a drug called cocaine and it's very expensive." "Really?" I said, "then the Delprados must be trillion Aires. I saw fields and fields of it."

"Ok, little brother. I believe you, but if I were you, I would say nothing about this to Dad. Tomorrow, I want you to show me these fields you saw, Ok." I said, "Yes" and then told him where they are located on the rancho and that it stretched for longer than the eye could see. Little did I know, what I was telling him!

I could not sleep a wink that night! Dad and Cliff were here and all I could think about was how I wanted to impress them with Mexico. I awoke to the smell of Grandmother's famous poyo and papas. It's chicken and potatoes smothered with onions and eggs. I beat everyone to the table. I ate so fast!

My father said, "if you don't slow down, you will have a tummy ache. Why are you in such a hurry?" "I just want to show you so much today." "My son, we will be here for at least 2 months, so don't worry. You will have time to show me everything.

When I heard two months, I felt so happy to know that Cliff will be here for so long. The bell rang and it was one of the ranch hands to take us to the rancho.

On the way to the rancho, my father asked the driver, if it is still the custom to only speak to the head of the family or has times changed? My Grandmother quickly answered, "We do not wish for change like Americans do and don't make me have to have a talk with you. You may be their father, but I am your mother and you will respect my customs." My father looked like a scolded child. I was learning that traditions here were handed down from generation to generation.

Here, in Mexico, fathers are more than just a provider. The fathers here, are the holder of the family's future. What is good for the father or Patron is good for the family. But my father still wanted to challenge it. "So, what you are telling me is that free thinking is not accepted here and that is why, I could never live here.

I will be polite and I will honor their Patron, but I will speak to whom I please and I will say as I feel. That was the first time I saw the defiance side of him. It seemed there was a Latin man inside him. When we arrived at the Rancho, my father had a look of not being impressed with what he saw. "I could buy 12 of these for what I paid for my house," he said.

We were greeted by Grandmother's brother. He was always glad to see her and very surprised to see my father and brother. "Hello my nephew, I have not seen you, since you were a child.

I am so proud of you. I hear from my son, how you kept this family running. I will never forget what you have done for us.

Let's go eat. I have had a brunch prepared with fruit, cheese, and champagne."

Later that day, Marcel leaned over and said, "I have some questions to ask you before you leave." I looked at him puzzled and shook my head. My mind started racing. What could he want to ask me? After we ate, Marcel Senior stood up and he asked my father to stand.

He explained to the family who my father was and how we are related. You could see that the family was surprised to hear that he refers to my father as the American Patron. I could tell my father was not happy with his new title because he interrupted Marcel and said, "I like to just be called Michael." Marcel Sr.'s face ran flushed with disgust. You could tell something was very different between these two men.

My Grandmother asked the Patron to tell us more about the fabulous rancho he has built for the family. He told her how it was an old cattle ranch that was going out of business and that he had purchased the ranch with the money Michael sent over the years.

He honored her honor by saying that her and her son had been more than a family member. He has been the only help, when there was no help. "Michael, you and your wisdom have given this family it's financial stability. Let me set the record straight, so everyone here will know.

I am the Patron, "Yes," but you are the founder of this family. Michael's, Wall Street education has been a great benefit to us. He has given this family well over $60,000.00 a year for the past 5 years. Thank you for being so generous and thank you Virginia for keeping us in your life. I thank your mother Michael for you, but my most prized possession is my son, Marcel Junior. My son was sick as a child and I had no money to take care of him.

You Michael, and only you, sent money, so I could give him the best care. You paid the hospital bills. You are a Saint to me. I have always seen you as a brother and a friend. I am in debt to you, Michael. Please never hesitate to ask this family for anything, because this is your family."

My father simply said, "You are welcome," and said to Grandmother, if I am anything, I am who I

am, because of this woman who has made me. I love you, Momma." We all held our glasses up and toasted Virginia.

Chapter 4
OUR PACT

Junior started in on me one day. "Hey DaVaughn, why is your padre so quiet?

He looks like a banker by the way he dresses, and if he is a Patron, like my padre where are his body guards? And what is Wall Street? Will someone please explain this place to me? What do they do there?"

"Hold on Primo, I said, one question at a time. You seem to like to make me answer multiple questions at one time." "I want to be like my rich American cousins, so I have to ask lots of questions," he said. "I have never met a Black American before and I have so many things to ask about your people.

But I know that you are aware of what my family is, and I want you to know you will be a full member, no matter what culture you are." When he said those words to me, I felt a feeling of pride and family. "Junior, we are not rich." "No, cousin" he said, you must be, because my father never gives that much praise. I knew your father sent us money and that he was a Black American; but after hearing my father speak of him, I know, he is a great man.

I owe you so much my cousin, and I want us to be like our fathers. I want us to forge a pact that we will never fight." We made that promise that very moment and I begin explaining to him who my father was. I told him how my father was an owner of a small corporation and he is well trained in securities and trading.

I told him that my father and my brother are the best I've ever seen. I told him why my father didn't need bodyguards. My father has never had those kinds of problems.

In the States, the courts handle things. I shared with him that I wished he did have them, because his father looks like a king when he leaves the house with the motorcade and the men with the guns. It looks like the movies. "I guess, Marcel Jr. said."

"My father has been shot twice and my mother" ......then he just stopped, so I didn't pry. I just changed the subject.

Now, my turn to ask a question, Junior. "Why does everyone have to listen to your father?" "Because in Mexico, he is the Patron. He guides the family. I want to be a policeman when I grow up, not a business man, but my father won't hear it and he guides the family. We are not allowed to be such men. My Poppa says the police are nothing more than over paid body guards and they are peasants to men like him."

I told him that my father has a lot of friends that are police and they are very rich men. "Never in Mexico," Junior said. "In Mexico, those men would be poor men." "Ok, enough questions," I said, save some for later.

Can we go to the fields? My brother thinks I am lying so I want to prove it to him. "Sure," Junior said, "as long as he keeps it to himself. Go get him and we can go walk the trails." As we started up the trails, Cliff asked Junior, if he has ever been to the states? Junior said, "I've been there as a baby, but never since then.

My father says it is a great place to make money, but the people are like the con men in Mexico City. They are dangerous and if

you turn your back on them, they will steal everything you have."
Cliff laughed and said, "He's kind of right, but it's not that bad.
You need to come to Washington D.C. That is the new Rome."
Junior smiled and said, "Rome I know, Caesar I know. Why do you
want to see the fields? Do you want to be a grower of coca leaves?"
Cliff answered like he always does. He tells you what you want
to hear. "I just want to see if my brother knows what he is talking
about." "No Cliff, it is true that the fields are as long as the eye can
see." "But how do you get water to the desert?" "There is water
under some parts of the desert. They find it with big pumps. We
are almost there. We have to go to another field because it is har-
vest time at the other."

We came upon this field that looked like a long train track. It
looked as if Cliff was about to faint because he squeezed my shoulder so tight, it hurt. Cliff said, "Do you to know how much money
we are looking at?" I looked at Junior with a blank look.

He seemed to have the same expression. "You goofs! It's maybe
six to seven million, that's not a lot of money!" Junior said, "Pesos?"

"No," Cliff said, "U.S. dollars!" Put it like this, if your father
owns this, he is the richest man in our family. I see now, why he is
the Patron. If I had this, I would be too! This was the beginning
of the end of Cliff.

One day before Cliff's departure back to the states, he told me
to call Junior and ask him if he would come spend the night at our
Grandmothers'. I knew Junior would say, yes, so I said, "He'll be
here. Why do you want to see him?" "To give him a present for
being such a great host.

He has shown me things, I only dreamed of," Cliff said. "Like
what?" I asked. The fields? "Yes, my little brother. Today our lives

have changed." The sound of his voice was a sound filled with mischief. Junior arrived around dinner time.

He explained that his father makes him eat with the family at every setting. My Grandmother had always taught me that it was the proper way for family. Cliff interrupted and said,

"For my last night in Mexico, I want to spend some time with my brother and my dear cousin."

Dad asked, "Where are you three going?" Cliff said, "Just for a walk downtown and maybe to Sanboms Restaurant for dessert. Matter of fact, we should go now, before it gets too late." We headed downtown toward the angel made of solid gold that's about twenty feet tall. It's pretty at night. We got to the steps of the statue and sat down.

"Do you know why I have asked to see you Junior? It is because, I want to make you part of your American family. Your father has been so kind to me. I feel like I am part of your family and I see that you will be the next in line to take your father's place as I will take my father's position.

I want you and DaVaughn to become close.

He lives here with you, so he will be my mouth piece. I have thought a long time about this and I am clear about this one thing, we will do big things! Junior answered with a scratchy voice, "Cliff, you are loved here in Mexico and this is your home away from home. Please don't be a stranger, but I do want to know one thing.

Why did you want to see the fields and how can they help you?"

"Junior, those fields are worth a lot of money to us. Those fields produce a drug that is known in the states as crack. It is made from the coca plant."

"So, you are telling me my father is a narco trafficanti?" Cliff looked at me, I looked at him, and the look we gave Junior, told him what we dare not say. "This is what the Romans call a Pax Romana. Together, my little cousin, we will shake the city of Washington D.C. I need you and my brother to find me the coca. It has to be someone you can ask, Junior?" "I will talk to my grandfather. He would never tell my father what we speak of."

"My plane leaves tomorrow. I will miss you two. Stay close to each other until I see you again. Accept my hand in friendship." "Patron, you and your brother are so dramatic. I am Junior, your cousin, and if one day I am the Patron, I will always be your cousin Junior."

Then he gave Cliff a hug. Junior said to Cliff, "We have a common friend in your brother. He is my best friend and I can see how you love him. Let us make him, should you say, our stick of reasoning.

If ever we should disagree, we will let DaVaughn decide in all fairness for both parties.

Do you agree DaVaughn?" I agreed.

"Cliff," Junior said, "you are a smart man and you are going to be a great family leader." When Junior said that, I could not help but feel ill because Cliff would run our family and Junior his. All I could think was, what about me?

Junior started to explain how Mexico runs. It seemed to be the perfect match. They wanted to know what the other knew. "I would like to have a rancho one day," Cliff said. "You have one," Junior said. So, do not want what you already have or it will drive you mad."

My brother also wanted bodyguards. Junior explained why they needed them to keep the government from just doing whatever it wanted to do to you. Cliff said, "We need them too. Not for that reason, but it would be nice to have them. Then we will one day have them for all of us!" Junior, "is it true that some kingpins own entire cities and more?" "Yes, they buy hospitals for the poor and protect widows and even help elect presidents and they do it for the people.

Here cartel members have generals in their pockets. In my town, there is a story that goes like this. There was this man who reported to the government that the cartel had taken over his town. The government sent three tank divisions to investigate the people in the town.

They thought they came to liberate them from the cartel, but the tanks started destroying their town, killing 15,000 people. The town only had 15,000 in it. There was no one left to complain. They even killed the animals by poisoning the cattle! It was all over the news.

The government made it look like a narco raid, so in little cities outside the region, it is well respected and known as the law never ever goes against the cartel. Not only will they kill you, but they will kill everyone in the town. The cartel believes that if you harbor a big mouth, then they will close every mouth in the town and wipe your town off the face of the earth." "I see, I said.

I read about that before. The Germans did it. Together we can do anything and with disunity, we can do nothing was their motto. As I thought about it, I thought that Junior would have the worse job in the world, because you don't get fired, you get killed! Maybe I was better off not being like them.

Chapter 5
TIME TO ROLL!

Christmas came that year and that's when we got the wheels rolling. Cliff called and said, "I am sending you a new video game. It's a Coleco vision." It was the new game out at that time in those days. Atari was the only game out, not like now-a-days where a game comes out every Christmas. "I don't know what for. The electricity is a different format here. It won't work here," but before I could finish, he said, "That's Ok, because you won't be keeping it." "Then, why send it, you goof?"

"Listen DaVaughn, he said, I will send it to you, and you will send it back to me. Have you spoken to Junior about what I need? Did he ask his grandfather?" "Yes, he told me to tell you that his Uncle will help us, but that you must take complete responsibility for every part of getting it to the states.

He also said that they only sell five at a time." I could hear Cliff sigh, "Five! I don't have that kind of money. DaVaughn, did he say how much?" "Eighteen thousand was the number Junior gave. It is for all five and he also told me that it was straight from the field." "You are shitting me, Cliff said. I am going to send you a cashier check in the mail, but only give it to them, if they give you what I want. No other deal is to be made, you understand?"

"I do Cliff; but down here, everyone has a gun, if he wants it,

31

he'll take it from me and there is nothing I can do about it." "I understand little brother. Be careful. I love you. Call me when you get it. Try to get it as fast as you can. Goodbye, little brother."

Two weeks later, I came home from school and there was a package on the table and an envelope. My Grandmother asked, "What has your brother sent you?"

I told her, he said he was going to send a video game for me and Junior to play with. "Oh, she said. I know you and Marcel Jr. will have fun with it."

"May I go see him?" "Yes, you may."

You just have to be on your best behavior and always offer to help the Patron of the house. He is very fond of you. Junior seems to be a little devilish. I don't want you to let him get you into trouble. "Ok, yes, Senior a. I give you my word, no trouble."

Friday evening came and I heard the car honk for me. As I was leaving, my Grandmother reminded me of my promise to not get into any trouble. I ran so fast to the car, I almost tripped coming out the door. I jumped into the car and chuckled a little because Junior acts the same way. It seems we make each other happy to see one another. He peeked out from the other side of the car. He had been hiding outside the car. "Hey Primo," he said at the top of his voice.

We hugged and then I told him about the money.

"I have the money for uncle." "Oh, that is so good. They will see I can be counted on. It's our first deal. I'm so happy. What's the other news?" "He also sent me this video game to put everything in."

"Damn, Junior said, your brother is smart.

I would have never thought of that." "You will one day," I

said. "Don't worry, hanging with Cliff, you can't help it." "Does the game work? No. It is an American game, so it won't format to the electricity here. I will give it to my grandfather and he will do the rest."

We arrived at the house and Junior fetched his grandfather. I went in and sat in the Patron's office. My uncle came in with a big grin on his face. He gave me a big hug and said, Mucho Gusto, Senior." It means many greetings. "Junior tells me you have something for me." "Yes Sir," I said. "No, DaVaughn, call me Uncle. It makes me feel good. Are my two little Patrons, ready to do what needs to be done?" "Yes, we are ready!

We will get up early tomorrow and handle your brother's business." "Where is the payment?" "I have it, I said, but I can't give it to you until I have what I came for. I was instructed to tell you this from my brother." My uncle said that he understood and that my brother was right to teach me this way.

He must have seen the fright in my face. "In Mexico, he said, no one can be trusted. What will we be using for the transport?" I showed him the game. "Your brother has a knack for this. I can tell he will go far, thinking like this."

The next morning came and I awoke to a tugging at my sheets. It was grandfather. "Let's go, he said, we will meet Junior at the other end of the rancho." Me and uncle started on the trail. We walked maybe twenty minutes until we saw Junior waving. He was standing with two ranch hands with rifles in their hands.

Suddenly, my body ran cold! Guns, money, and Mexicans! You add it up! All of the news I see here, can't be lying about the Cartel. "Good morning grandson," my uncle said.

We all jumped in the jeep and started up a different trail. I asked Junior, "Where does this trail lead?" "I don't know. I never been up this one." Again, the cold feeling ran through me. Soon, we came to these two trees with markings on them.

I asked my uncle, "What do the markings mean?" He began to tell me that it means several things. He told me that the first marking tells you whose land you are on, and the second, he explained, is a Cartel symbol. It says leave now or be killed.

As he was talking, my uncle motioned one of the guards to retrieve something from inside the tree. He stuck his hand in and out came five kilos. Later, we would install them in the game. "Don't worry DaVaughn," my uncle said, grabbing my knee in an assuring way. "Now, may I have my payment?" I handed him the envelope and he handed me the bag with the bricks. "I'm sorry for being so cautious." "Don't worry, he said. I am so proud of you two, I could cry. Today, you two are men."

We got back to the house before Junior's father called for breakfast. "I will have the hands, install this right now," Uncle said. "What time will you be leaving?" "On Sunday, I replied. Early. Grandmother likes me home early." "No problem," he said. Then he left. 'How much do you think your brother will pay us for our part in this?" Junior asked.

"Don't worry. Cliff is a great guy. He will be fair." I got home early like I said.

I ran in the house and called Cliff. It was nine o'clock at night. "Hey little brother; he said, I am so happy to hear from you, I have it." The scream he let out could wake the dead. "I have it. It's in my room as we speak." "Is it heavy? Does it smell?"

I answered, no, to all his questions. He said, "Listen carefully.

I want you to put it back in the box I sent it in and then I want you to find the strongest tape you can find. The box has a return to sender postage already prepaid. Just have Grandmother take it to the Embassy and put it in the mail."

"Cliff, what is my payment for all of this?" "I will send you and Junior something as soon as I get the game back." The next morning, I told Grandmother that the game did not work and Cliff said to send it back, so he could send me a new one. The return postage is already paid. I just need to stick it in the outgoing mail at the Embassy. I phoned Cliff as soon as she left to let him know it should be there four or five days from now.

"Plan, well done, little brother, and keep your mouth shut and cross your fingers. When I get that package, it will change our lives and dad will have to respect us now in a different way. Thank Junior and Uncle for me." Ok Cliff. Call me when it gets there."

"Will do, and we got off the phone. I sat on my bed and thought to myself. I had just done my first deal ever in life and it was for 5 kilos of some drug, I had never seen before. Wow, times were changing fast for us. We were now, in some ways, a part of the cartel and neither of us knew what we had just done to our lives.

Chapter 6
WHAT I'M GOING TO BE

My school was like a mini campus. It was full of privileged children. You could only go to this school, if you were rich or some dignitary's kid. There were a lot of kids there that had "family money" as they called it. I would go around and just ask my fellow classmates where they were from, and the answers they gave would be some of the richest countries in the world.

Chile, Russia, and Spain were where most of them whispered. Their dads were doctors or lawyers. My favorite was, an international business man. My father was a well to do man, but we do not vacation in Rome. I found it funny that all they wanted to know was about America and what it is like.

I became the American friend who could get them blue jeans, sneakers, and music. You would be surprised at how the urban culture has infiltrated the world. Who would think Run DMC could be heard in the middle of Mexico City. I got questions like, have you ever been to a rap concert? Or, have you ever met a rapper? They acted like rappers are on every street corner.

One day I was sitting in my Spanish class and I heard, "Senior Kidd, we will be talking about what we all want to become and I feel that by you being an African American with Spanish roots, I think you should have a lot to say." I stood from my seat and said with a scratchy voice, "I want to be a rancher like my uncle. "A rancher?"

"Yes, I like the lifestyle, the guards, the motorcade, the respect you get from your family, and the most important thing to me in my life, is I want to be powerful." The teacher gave me a look that could cut ice, like I said a bad word. "Senior Kidd, she said, a rancher usually does not have body guards and they don't make a lot of money, plus you spoke of power. What would you do with your power?"

"I would feed the hungry in

Mexico, educate the poor, and make the rich listen to the poor. That is using power wisely." Her face now had a smile that said, 'I see now that you have a dream' and it gave me hope.

When I arrived home, it was cold, unlike what most people think, it does get a little nippy in Mexico. I went straight to my room to lie down.

My Grandmother yells to me that Cliff had called twice today. He wanted me to call as soon as I got in. I picked up the phone and dialed with a shaky hand. I feared that the package did not make it there, so I held the phone close to my ear, so my Grandmother would not hear Cliff screaming.

The phone rang twice and then that's when I heard Cliff say, "You, my brother, are a rich man, you and Marcel! A letter is on its way. It has three checks in it. One for you to put in your trading account and the other two are for Junior and his father. Give it to Uncle. Hell, give the Patron his. I am so proud of you, DaVaughn.

You have made me so happy. I owe you a lot. We will be together forever. Guess what, my little brother? I am going to school to learn more about trading commodities. I will follow Dads' footsteps. Now I have the money and the power to do what I want without his control.

You must come to visit me soon. I miss my little brother, sometimes. When the envelopes get there, call me." "Yes Cliff, I will call when they hit my hands." Cliff seemed different somehow. I just thought it was the money. Six days later, the envelope came. I nearly tore it in half trying to open it.

It was three cashier's checks, each made out in the amount of twenty-thousand dollars. I was holding sixty thousand in my hand. I got dizzy.

I sat in the chair and just giggled a while like a mad man. I ran to the phone and after I got myself together, I phoned Junior. "I must see you. Skip dinner and tell your father that my Grandmother needs your help. He will let you come." "Should I bring some of the ranch hands? Are you Ok? "No, you just come," and we hung up the phone.

Marcel got to the house about seven. "Ok, Primo, I'm here. What's the big deal? My dad was mad that I was not going to be at the table."

I walked up to him and gave him a hug and said, "For you Patron." I handed him the envelopes.

He smiled and said, "Stop playing, I am no Patron." He opened the envelopes and he looked at the checks the same way I did. I saw sweat form on his brow. He jumped clear out of his boots and asked, "This is mine?" "Yes, one is for you and tell Uncle, my brother said, "this is for the Patron." I think you should give it to him yourself, Junior said, why should my grandfather get the credit for our idea?" I agreed that I would deliver it myself. "Do you want me to mention you?" "Yes, but just say I helped. Don't mention my payment. I will now show you how to invest like we do in the markets. I will call Cliff and he will tell me where to put our money." "Ok, yes cousin, I will do what you want.

We are going to line up a future for ourselves. My dad says a Black man has to do more than just work. He says, he has to play the game of money on Wall Street. I am going to write my dad and ask him to send me my old notes on trading. He keeps everything.

You gave my family something, now I will repay the favor to you." I hugged Marcel again and as he left, he looked at me and said, "Don't say Black man to me again. You are a man. I have read about what the white man did to your people." I said.

"Don't forget your people too. The world is a bad place. He seemed to be hurt that I would say such a thing to him, so I said to pep the mood, I reminded him of today and now and our money, each with twenty-thousand. "You should get back before your dad sends the troops." We both laughed and he got on the elevator. As the doors closed, I felt like I had finally done something right. Boy, was I ever wrong to think such a thing.

The first lesson on Wall Street seemed to bewilder Marcel, so I tried to use things he knew, like cattle and gold. "Ok Marcel, I have to be honest. Stocks are like the wind. You never know which way they will blow. You just have to do your homework.

I think this will help you. This is a small overview of Wall Street. Wall Street was created by the government and the railroad tycoons like men named JP Morgan, a Rail Road Mogul." "Excuse me, what is a mogul?" "Let's say the Patrons of Patrons." "Oh, I see, he said, the Domo!" "Yes, and for you who don't know what Domo is, it is the title given to the head of all the cartels. Most corporations are represented on Wall Street.

The New York Exchange is the first Exchange, then Chicago. Get it? I told him that there are multiple exchanges in America and several indexes, but we will get to that later. We were going to focus on the corporations. I taught him about how railroads, telephone companies and land development companies started the Exchanges. I shared with him that my dad always says IBM is the sure bet when she is running well and real estate, oil and cattle too.

My uncle had been educating me on it and I follow the sector on Wall Street. I showed how one thing applies to another and so on and so on. "I got it, but cousin, how do you make money?" "Pay attention. Get a piece of paper. Let's say, you have your own cattle company and you find people to give you money to buy more cattle and to make the business grow.

You then take some of the money and apply for a loan at a bank. You take the loan and apply it to company progress that could be buying better stocks, buying up competition, or just making every part of the business more efficient. You with me so far cousin? Well, if you look at it closely, you have a business with investors which means money and a loan which still means money, so you see, there is the money."

I could see he was not clear, so I went another route. "We have a business, (I pointed to his notes), we have money from people and we have to buy cattle for the business." I could see the light go on in his head because he asked, "When I go get the loan, I can do whatever I want with the loan money?" "Yes, I said, as long as it is better for the company.

That leads me to the next lesson. Most companies take the money they make from cattle sales and invest in another company, totally different from itself, so I don't see why you could not. What business would you get into? (Like I didn't know what his answer would be) "The coca business." "I know, you goof. I was being funny." We both laughed. "I once took all my birthday money and put it on this stock I saw my dad talk about.

I gave him my money, he bought the shares, and I waited and I watched the stock.

There was this toy company that made this toy that everyone wanted to have, so I figured, how could I lose. Long story short, I spent fifty dollars on the stock and when it was summer, my dad gave me a thousand dollars. I have been hooked since.

A company issues shares out to the public and its staff. Twenty dollars is the number I want you to write down. I have it with new investors buying up the stock. The twenty jumps to twenty-five.

Now underline the twenty, so you will know where we started. So, we made a five-dollar profit! He said, "I'm not stupid. Ok, so how can I lose?" "A company can have any number of reasons it can fail and when people hear bad news, they don't invest. You lose, if you do not sell your shares before the bad news. You can even lose the shares if the company goes under, so be careful of what you invest in. Do your homework."

"How many companies can you invest in at one time, Marcel asked?" "As many as your pocket will permit, but remember, never put all your eggs in one basket." "Huh?" "Why buy one golden bull if you can't buy the cow? He has to mate too. More can sometimes be bad." "I get the drift. It seems so confusing.

I'm glad I have you DaVaughn." "We are going to start you off with two companies my dad gave me to start with, IBM and gold. He gave me fifty shares. It split twice, which means that the company says, I will give you two shares that will equal the one share you have."

"How is that good?" "It is good when the company moves the stock up again. "Oh, I see!" "Well, I now have 200 shares of a company just because of the splits." "This is a lot to remember. I think it is best if you do my investing for me cousin. You seem to have a clear understanding about these matters. Tell me, who is this Dow Jones?

I hear it on the news every night, but I don't know who he is. They never show him." I laughed so hard. He could tell, he asked a blundering question. "He was a man who could calculate how the markets would do by averaging key sectors of the United States economy.

He could forecast the overall financial status of the whole country. That's why it's called the Dow Jones Average named after the man who came up with a good system to measure the United States economy." "Does Cliff invest his money this way?"

"Yes, the whole country does, if they want to be rich. At least that's what my dad tells me." "I will listen to you cousin, because I know nothing of these things. "They don't teach you things like this in my school and I want to invest in the company you spoke of. What must I do?"

I told him to have grandfather open up a trading account through his bank. Then he could buy the share on your behalf and I would tell my uncle when to buy it. All he had to do was just open the account. "I will help you and your brother, he said. I can get us all the product we want. You guys take over from there, Ok."

I agreed. "You know, Marcel, there is a saying in the states. "They say you will either lead or be led. I can see, we are leaders. My father tells me that Mexico is a dangerous place for a man who wants to speak his mind. He says that, "If you don't listen to the

Patron, he can order you to be killed." "Is this true?" Marcel shook his head and said, "Yes, we all listen, so don't worry about that." "Has your father ever killed anybody, Marcel?"

"We are not allowed to speak of such things, so let this be your first lesson from me. I will answer your questions because you are my brother, but you will get yourself in trouble asking such things. Take my advice. Just don't ask about these types of things. I will tell you this. I had uncles on my mother's side of the family.

They are all dead now, and it is said that my father had them killed. All I know is that one by one they were killed. My father would tell me, "We are not like these men. They did not respect family and they would not listen to the Patron. A man who does not listen to his Patron is better off dead and should be." I thought I was schooling Marcel, but he just taught me a lesson of a lifetime!

Chapter 7
BANISHED

I got to come home once out of my four years of being banished. I say banished, because that's what it felt like for so long. I missed my mom a lot during the time we were apart.

Mexico was having some bad things happen, so my Grandmother thought it was best for me to go back to the states. She told me that a bad man is targeting Americans and the U.S Embassy.

She told me that she would send for me when it was over and that I would be leaving as soon as possible, so start thinking about what I wanted to pack. "Excuse me Grandmother, I am unclear. You never said the name of the man causing this trouble." "His name is Mor Ma Kadifi. He is a terrorist.

He has waged war on all Americans. He blew up a hotel that was across the street from the Embassy where I work. It killed 58 people at one time and wounded our culture.

So, you see, I have no choice but to send you back. Be good for me like you are with me here." Again, I smiled. I called Marcel and told him the news and I could tell he took it hard. I told him, don't worry because I would write once a week and I will address it to the driver, so his dad won't get wind of what we are doing.

"Will you open a trading account for me in the U. S. and a

savings account?" "Sure, I said. If I hear of any good stocks to buy, I will let you know."

We also agreed that one kilo a month would be shipped to me. Marcel would have to now deal with the shipping arrangements and I would send something to ship it in, was my end of the deal. Marcel told me he had a surprise for me. He wouldn't tell me what, but he did say, it will blow my mind.

I came home to the states in the summer of 1989. It seemed to me, that everything had changed. I stepped off the plane and it felt like a different world to me. My father picked me up from the airport in a new 500 Sel Mercedes. "Wow Dad, I said, this is a nice car."

"Thanks son, I have so many of my toys to show you, with a wink in his eye and a smile. I bought a new house for two hundred thousand and turned it into a million-dollar profit. How savvy is that, Sonny?" "Real savvy, Poppa. "So now that you are home what do you think of the Delprados Patron, Marcel, and the ranch life?" "I love it.

It is a great life. They live like movie stars. We have so much to do on the ranch, bull fights, horses, races, cock fights, and dog fights. When I'm at the ranch, we have bodyguards that stay in eyesight of Junior and I.

When we go into town, it's like being a star. People move when we come down the street. I would live there, if I could and never leave." My father seemed to be irritated with my response, by what he said next.

"Son, he needs bodyguards for his safety. You do realize people are trying to kill him? I hate that your Grandmother takes you around them, but she argues, you cannot run from your heritage.

I'll tell you this Sonny boy, I have more money than Don Marcel and if he were in this country, he would be in jail for the life that he chose.

You seem a little plump to me. We will work on your weight while you are here." Does Cliff know I'm here?" "Of course, he does. He has a big surprise for you. I'm sure he has told you. He has been working on it for some time now." "What is it Poppa?" "I can't tell you son. Just wait you'll see!"

I went to see my friends whom I had not seen in years. My final stop was my brother's house. Dad gave him our old house on First Street, Northwest.

It was a nice house, but it seems the neighborhood was a scene from a bad movie. I walked up the steps and rang the bell.

My father yelled, "Remember, you don't want to disappoint your Grandmother. Be good. She told me to remind you." "I will Sir," and I turned and rang the bell. Cliff opened the door and you could tell he was happy to see me. I have always loved my brother. He was the world to me and I could tell, I was his world too.

We entered the living room where there was a table full of food and all of my cousins were there! Antone, Eric, Rick Rick, Clip, Danny, everyone was there! It was like a mini family reunion. All this was for me! Cliff said, "You earned this and more. Here, little brother."

He handed me a bag filled with ten thousand dollars and a set of car keys. He walked me out to the back of the house with everyone following behind us. "Ok, he said, close your eyes." I did, and when I opened them, there was a new sports car.

They told me it was a 300 ZX. It was a nice ride, but I was scared, because I didn't know how to drive and I didn't have a license. "We will teach you and you do have a license." He gave me an ID with the name of someone I didn't know, but it had my picture on it.

"Little brother, I'll always dot your I's and cross your T's. You have a job this summer. I thought, why would I need a job, if I have a bag full of money? But I just listened. "The job pays $3,000 a day. You can make more or less. We will see how you do." "Wow, thank you everyone, I said!" "No, thank you," Antone said, "without you and your Mexican cousin, none of this would be possible." "When do I start guys?"

"When we get back from Jamaica," Cliff said. "I am taking you there. We are driving to Florida and we will charter a boat to the island." "Why don't we fly?" "Because Antone has a prison record. He can't get a Visa, so he will be smuggled into Jamaica and then back to the U.S. We will be in Jamaica illegally." "Ok, everyone, I said, thanks for everything, but I would like to speak to Cliff alone for a minute."

Cliff and I were finally alone. "I am so proud of you, little brother. You have done more for me than dad could ever do. I have your new uniform to put on. You look like a Mexican with those clothes on." He handed me a jacket with rhinestones and the state of Texas painted on it, a set of white Gucci tennis shoes, a white Gucci T shirt and 9 pairs of jeans.

There were so many clothes in the spare room. I couldn't believe all of those clothes were mine. If Marcel could see this, he would shit on himself. "We have to send some of this stuff to Marcel."

"Ok, little brother, we will. Here is your protection. It's a 22-caliber hand gun. It should be enough for you and here is a bullet proof vest. Pray you never need it. Mine has saved me twice, so wear the damn thing anyway." "Where did you get this?" "Dad owns a security company. "What can I say, if things get lost?" He laughed. The laugh was not the problem I thought, it's what will dad do to us, if he ever finds out?

I received a call one day at my mom's. It was Marcel. "Hello, Primo. I got your mom's number from your Grandmother. I have been going by, checking on her for you. Do you think Senior Michael will let me come visit you in the states?" "I'm sure he will cousin. Will your father let you come, is the question?

I was just telling my father how much I love being on the rancho and how much we do together."

"The Patron is coming to the states, but he doesn't want me around while he is doing business, so he wanted to see how you felt about me spending some time with you, while he was in the states?"

"This is good, now you get to live, my friend, and I mean live! I will show you things in Washington D. C. you will never see in Mexico. You will love it here. It's got everything you would like.

I have my own gun now, Marcel. Will your father be bringing some of his guards with him?"

"No, Marcel said, it attracts too much attention in the states. Can you do me a favor, DaVaughn?

I want to send you something, so send me a game like before and I will handle the rest. What address can I send it to?" "Cliff has a P.O. Box we can use." I heard the phone buzzer go off, so I knew that the conversation was over.

"I will call again soon cousin." Then the phone went dead. I thought, it must be hell, to only be able talk on the phone for ten minutes at a time.

I phoned my dad to tell him the news and he agreed, with no hesitation. "Sure, he said, it will be good for him to see the real world. Is his father coming? I said, "He will be coming, but not staying."

I could hear the irritation in his voice. "Do you like the Patron? "I love him, Sonny. I just don't agree with his lifestyle. It costs so many people so much for him to be a Patron. Juniors' father thinks he is better than me, because he is surrounded by killers all day.

I could not live like that son. I would never want you to live like that either. In Mexico, a man does not have the right to make his own mind up.

He must obey his clan leader at all times. What a life, never able to think for yourself. What a waste! Do you know why it is this way, Sonny? It is because men like Marcel teach the family that there can only be one man in charge of a family.

The one who commands, is the one for the job. I send money to him because your Grandmother says, we owe it to the family to help them to become like we are in America. But Sonny, "know this, he is not rich.

He just lives in a country where the dollar goes much further. Marcel is the only one on that side of the family with the hunger to be a Patron.

If I send thirty-thousand to him, it turns into three hundred and fifty thousand pesos. That's a lot of money in his little town. So, you see? He is the only man with that type of cash in the town.

Remember this Sonny; his family believes in killing each other off, to gain control of his power, so he has a tough job. If you don't listen to me, I just go around you. With Marcel, you die. That's it.

Do try to remember, that I am the real Patron of that family. It is my money that feeds his power base. Tell Junior, he can come whenever he wants, but you are his keeper. I don't want any problems out of Don Marcel."

He said that with a chuckle.

Two months went by and then I got a call. The voice on the other end was screaming so loud. "I'm here, you chinga. My father said to tell your dad to send a car." "We drove ourselves here Marcel. I will come and get you with Cliff. What airport are you at?"

"We are at Dulles. Hurry, Primo. I have so much to tell you." I hung up the phone and called Cliff to tell him, we have to pick up the Patron. Cliff answered in disbelief. "The Patron is here?" "Yes, Marcel too." "I'm on my way. Tell them that a limo will be there to get them."

"I just told them we were coming, Cliff." "My little brother, a man like Patron Marcel does not ride in a regular car. It would be an insult to him. I'll deal with it. See you in a minute."

August 26, 1992, I woke up as I usually do, got dressed, and headed up to the roof to have breakfast. My father loved to eat breakfast on the terrace. My father was doing his regular thing, talking on the phone and reading the business section of the newspaper. I gestured to him from the sliding door as to say, should I leave or stay for his phone conversation.

He motioned me in and told me to listen closely. "Dan, he said, I want a fifty-thousand share position on this stock. I feel it is a winner." Dan was my dad's broker. He was a real nice guy, they went to school together and have stayed friends ever since then.

"Dan, I know how you feel about large positions for long lengths of time, he said, but this I feel is the one. My son is at the table. I will call you when I get in the office. See Sonny, to make money you have to spend money. I use this attitude, Sonny.

I see a stock I like and I study it. I buy it, then I sell it for a profit. Use these principles and you can't go wrong in the markets. Have you been saving some of your summer money up?" I wanted so bad to say, I have so much money I don't know what to do with it all, but I just agreed and kept eating. "Dad, what company were you talking about to Dan?"

"Son, I have been reading about these new tech companies and this one company looks like it has the right product and the right people in place to make a profitable company. The name of the company is Microsoft.

All I know Sonny was, I was at a meeting downtown having lunch with the Mayor's office and they were discussing what the new computer systems would run on.

I kept hearing the Mayor reference the company to the panel, as to say, I have made my choice and this will be the company the District government will be awarding the bid too. So, I did the math. It's over ten thousand employees in the government. That means fat profits for the company that gets the contract.

I've heard rumors too that there was this guy in the computer industry that would change how we all use our email addresses again. Do you know how many people use email? Chi-Ching is all I could say! I found out that this guy was submitting contracts all over the country.

For this software, the District government alone wrote a check for ten million. Long story short, my son, I think you should put your summer savings here. You and your brother are old enough to trade without my signature, so tell him what I said.

Your summer savings should go to the portfolios. No ifs, no buts, you hear me?" "Yes sir, I said."

"And since you work for me, I would like a five-page report on this company."

I just agreed. Here is the name again, Microsoft, and the man who owns it is, Bill Gates. Use this to track down company information. I want a full scope on this company." "You can count on me Dad."

"Now Davaughn, keep Marcel out of trouble. I hear he likes to hang in some rough places. Don't take him to the bad spots. Show him the good rich places to go party. Do you know what Marcel Sr. said to me yesterday? He said that I live in a hubble and if you have to drive yourself, how do you enjoy the car?

And this one really ticked me off, he said that if he were running my company, he would turn it into a cartel holding. Do you know what that means? It means, his funny money would be funneled through my company to clean it up.

You do know what that means of course? I do want to know why Cliff is the topic of every conversation. It's Cliff this, Cliff that. I don't like it, but if I ask your brother, he will just say I'm being over protective, so you keep me informed, my little bird."

Trying to change the subject, I said, "I'm so proud of him being in college, isn't that good?" "Son, apples are apples and oranges are oranges. You just let me know if you see something I should know." With that said, he stood up and kissed me on the forehead, leaving me at the breakfast table.

I got a page around ten and it was Junior. I could tell by the code he used it was him. Our phone number to my Grandmothers' house in Mexico was his code. "I have a problem he said, when I called, my package never showed. What do you think I should do cousin?" I thought, what can we do? Going and asking for a hot package is not the brightest thing to do. "Give it some more time." I could tell he was scared. I got the feeling the package was not all his.

Several days went by before we got a call from the post office telling us we had to come get the package because we missed the delivery. I drove Marcel to pick up the package. I told him I will go in and get it, but if he sees anything funny, just get the hell out of here. I walked in the post office and looked around to see if I could see any undercover police. I held my breath the whole way to the counter.

There was no one in line, so I just walked up. "Excuse me sir, I have a package to pick up." "Your name son?" "DaVaughn and here is my ID." He closed the sliding glass, so I could not hear what he was saying. I started to get nervous, then he came back to the glass and said that he had had the package under his desk for a week. "I am so glad to see it leave. Sign here and she is all yours." "Thank you, Sir."

I walked out the door so fast, I almost fell on my way back to the car. Junior jumped out the car and started running towards me. "I did it, he said. I did it! My first smuggle and it worked like clockwork. Your brother should get an award for this idea." I heard him, but I was so scared. I was just waiting for the police to jump out and yell, you're under arrest, but it didn't happen. We ran to the car.

Once in the car, I told Marcel that I needed him to keep me informed about my brother." "He won't tell me how far he is in this business, but I know he will want to show off for the Patron. "See if you can find out for me."

"For you cousin, I will do this, but I don't like it. It is being a rat and I don't like it. I know you are trying to protect your brother and I will do this for you. Give me some time and I will have some information for you."

I dropped Marcel off with the package at his fathers' hotel. "Hey Primo, I will have your half this evening. Come and get it or I will send it to you by carrier." I just nodded and went off to do what I was growing to love, making money and it was by way of Coke.

Coke was the "in thing" to do, it seemed at the time. I noticed it had a violent streak in the business, but the money seemed to be worth the risk. My theory to selling coke was simple to me.

I never wanted to get caught with it on me, so I made two hundred dollars a day, which isn't a lot in the business. I saw it like this, that's less than a quarter which can only land you a small stay in jail, if caught as a juvenile.

You do the math. Three hundred-and-sixty-five-days times one hundred dollars is a nice end of the year bonus and I still had one hundred dollars a day to live on. It worked for me. With a check from work, to make it look good to my father, it was the perfect plan to me.

I can remember my first hot day when I changed to this plan. I had just done about two hundred rocks that morning.

How good of a day is that, at fifty dollars a rock! I should have been happy with that, but when greed is involved, you never have enough. I went back to my brothers' stash apartment and stashed my cash and got my second round of rocks for the night.

It was still on a block, so I had to chop my rocks up into fifties. Being impatient, I thought I will just chop up in the back seat of my car. How stupid was that? But money blinds your judgment.

What was I thinking, that I had a license to sell coke? I got back around First Street and it was still going.

There were lines of coke fiends. I parked my car on the back side of the block, so I could see if the police were coming up the street. I pulled out my mini digital scale and got to work bagging up. It is tedious, but it pays. Boy, does it pay! With my hand catching a cramp, I saw an unmarked car go by.

I didn't think anything of it, because it kept going, but then I noticed it was backing up to my car. I threw the coke I had on my lap out the door, but I could not get out fast enough and get the keys out of the car. At first, I thought I should make a run for it then, I thought, you idiot the car is registered to Cliff.

Better deal with this myself. The fat cop could barely get out the car. "So, what you doing here?" Oh, look-a-here, coke, my favorite thing to lock people up for. Hands on the car, Sonny. Whose car is this?"

"It's mine." "Yours, huh? Well, let's just see. Call it in, partner. I bet its stolen.

You have ID, son? "Yes sir, it's in my pocket." Reaching for his gun he said, "I want you to retrieve your ID slowly and don't make a mistake. I would hate to shoot you, son." I was placed in the back of the car.

One of the officers got in the car and said, "we know you and we know your brother and his crew. We have been watching you guys and guess what, you just gave us a way into the gang. I left a message on your brother's car. I guess he didn't get it.

Well, you, my son, are being arrested for crack cocaine and will be booked at the First District. Here is a phone. Give your brother a call. Tell him I have little, baby bear in custody and if he doesn't come to answer some questions, you are going to jail." "I can save you the trouble officer. All he will say is, why are you calling me? I don't know what you're talking about. You are better off just letting me call my dad." We got to the station and I was booked with having one ounce of crack with the intent to distribute.

Because I was a juvenile, they put me in this empty room and hand cuffed me to the wall. I was there it seemed like forever, then the door flew open. It was the fat cop. "I am going to give you one more chance. Call your brother." "No sir. I think if you want to talk to him, you better catch him, ok?" "No, not ok.

You have the right to remain silent. You have the right to have an attorney. I stopped listening after that. I just tuned him out. After his big speech, he said the unimaginable. "Call your father. I want to speak with him."

All the courage I had, ran out of me. What my father was going to do to me, is all I could think about. I picked up the phone on his desk and began to call my dad's office number. It began to ring and with each ring, I felt like passing out right there.

The admin picked up, "Kidd Investment Corporation." "Hey, it's me Diane. I'm in a bit of a spot. I really need to speak to my dad?" "He isn't in. I will call around, but you know your dad may not even be in the country, as far as we know sometimes. I will do my best to find him. "Thanks, I said and asked, in a panic voice, tell my brother, I'm in jail, please."

I quickly hung up the phone. "So, it seems, Mr. Kidd, you are in a jam and I know just the place to put a spoiled brat like you." He led me to this elevator and we went up to the next floor. It opened to what look like a juvenile day care. I kept thinking in my mind, as I looked out from the elevator, that this was not for me.

"Please, don't rush Mr. Kidd." He must have seen the fear in my eyes. "You will really meet the world here."

He opened up the metal fence and gave me a shove inside it. "Enjoy. I will let you know when I hear from your father." I sat in the far corner, not to mix with the other inmates. If I were in Mexico City, I would never have been held this long just, because I am in the Delprado family. But this is the United States and the Delprados are "nobodies."

After a while, an officer came in with a clip board and he started yelling names one by one. Then I heard my name. "All of you gentlemen, he said, will be transported." I asked, where are we going?" "My friend, he said, you are off to court in the morning.

Then after court, you will probably be sent to a juvenile detention center. Where do you live?" "I live on Fourteenth Street, downtown." "Then you will be going to the facility in Northeast, the Montana facility. You better hope the arresting officer doesn't show for court because that place is filthy in all aspects of the word.

The next morning came and I was given a meal that tasted like warm air. The guy in the bunk next to me was chained to his bunk. "You must be a bad boy, I said.

Why the chains." He lifted his head and answered, "They say, I fight too much. I get in a fight at least ten times a day, so I guess, I do." He started laughing. "The CO tells me you are in here for dope." "Yeah, I got caught with some crack in my car. Not a good thing to have in the car. I see now."

"Homey, you will get ninety days. You are a juvenile. They don't have room to keep us long. Do you have a lawyer? If you do, then you just might be able to work your way out of it." "My brother will have one for me. I don't have to worry about that." "Will one of your parents be there?"

"Unforgivably, yes my dad will have to know about this." "Shit, he said, homey you going home. Must be nice. I'm here for ninety days and I'm just here. I got a couple of months to go."

Court time came and I was praying, dad would be there and that GOD would forgive me for being so stupid. Then it hit me. What will my Grandmother think? What will she do to me? The feeling of fainting again, came over me. The clerk called my name and I took my seat in front of the judge. The prosecutor began to read the charges.

The judge wondered if I had a lawyer and I nodded, yes. My dad was in the back looking through the glass. I saw him out the corner of my eye, giving me his look of disappointment. Things went so fast. I didn't say much, but by the time it was over, I was found not guilty, due to the officer taking his statement without my guardian's consent. Good Ole, Uncle Sam and his loopholes! Now came the real trial, I had to face my father.

I got in the car and didn't say a word. I could see the fury in his eyes. "Why would you do this to your future? Where have you learned this from?" I know, he said, those damn Delprados. I will make them pay. You watch! The well will run dry! Your Grandmother is so hurt.

She refuses to go out of the house. She feels responsible. Look what you have done with this crazy stunt." I was so afraid. I answered him like the son I was to him. "Poppa, I don't know why I did it. And the Delprados have nothing to do with it. And Cliff? He is going to kill me, so you see I am in a bad place in my life. I'm sorry. It will never happen again."

I looked out of the window trying not to cry, but I could not hold back the tears.

I hurt my Grandmother and she is the world to me. This train I am on is not traveling well and it's just the beginning.

Chapter 8
FAMILY IS EVERYTHING

A few weeks had gone by and Junior was well on his way, with Cliff helping him get rid of the stuff. He was in the best place, he thought. He had his own money and his father was nowhere around. But his balloon soon burst when he got a call from his father informing him that he would be there in two days and would be staying in Washington for a while. I got a frantic call from Junior. "My father is on his way and I need a place to hide the money.

Your brother is a good man at what he does, but what should I do with all the money I have? My father will be here soon and I have to get rid of it or I will be in big trouble. Cousin, I want you to stash it for me and I will just let you know, what I need." I said Ok, and asked how much, do you have to hide?

"I have about twenty-thousand in small bills. Please cousin, I can't get caught with this money. Come get it now." I agreed and went and got the money. It took both of us all day to fold each bill into small, like rolls. I unhooked the old radiator in my room and hid them inside the pipes.

I awoke one morning to a familiar voice echoing through the house. It was Don Marcel. He and my dad were having breakfast. "I need a favor Michael, he said, I am asking not as a cousin, but as a man trying to hold his family together. I have a stone in my shoe at home.

A young member of my enemy is planning to strike against my family, our family. I went to the Domo of my town and he gave me permission to take down the whole family against ours, but he wants ninety-thousand upfront. You are the Patron in America, so I come to you for help."

My dad hated flattery and he really hated for people to play on his emotions. He always told me that men should speak clearly and to the point and always respectfully. "Oh, I see now, you need more help," my father said.

"Yes, Michael, we will be crushed, if I do not get this money. I also need to leave Junior here with you. I don't want him caught in the middle of this war and your sons are great influences on him. I will only leave him with you because I know no harm will come to him as long as he is under your protection."

My father agreed that he would look after him. Then he called me into the room. "Sit down, Marcel has something to say to you. Junior will be staying here in the states. I would like you to keep an eye on him.

He has never been so free to do whatever he wants, so make sure he is choosing correctly. I know you love him like a brother and that you would not let him get in trouble. I know you understand his position. Junior is next to be the head of the family after me, so he can't get into trouble.

I know he tries to be the good, little bambino, but I know of the mischief he can get into too. He fears me as the Patron, not me, as his father. Keep him safe and I will make a place for your brother in my family. You would like to see him under me in some way?"

"Yes sir, I said, my brother away from the states working with you would fulfill both our dreams."

Then Marcel said, "Now please, tell your dad that I will be waiting for him in the study. As I left the room, I kept trying to figure out why my father had left the room. The study room was a cherry wood, stained room with French carvings in the wood. The back steps to the room led down to an old servants' corridor. I crept down the back steps, so I could hear what Don Marcel and my father were talking about.

My father was already in the room when Marcel knocked on the door. "Excuse me, Michael. I know how busy you must be." "No Marcel, what is on your mind?" "I will be leaving soon. I fear that if I stay too long, it will give my enemies time for ill plotting. I first want to say, thank you, for your hospitality. And second, I need to give you this. I bought a house while I was here.

This is the deed. Junior will live there. I am having it converted into three separate units, so I can generate rental profits. My son is totally at your disposal while he is here. Mike, he is not like DaVaughn. I must warn you, he wants to be a Patron and he knows he is my succession to run the family. I must say though, your mother, has done a fine job with your boy.

I wish mine would listen like yours. I want Junior to run the family after me because it is his right, but I'm scared he will not be able to control his greed. I see signs in him that stress me.

I wished he liked to make the money as much as he likes to spend it. He works hard on my rancho, but he won't go to school. I threaten, I beat him, and still nothing. It just makes him meaner. I hope whatever your son has, will rub off on him. I really like your kid.

He has a very good wit. My father stood up and said, "you might not think so after I tell you what he has done. He was arrested for having coke. I'm afraid to send him back, because I know he had to have gotten involved in Mexico." "Come now Mike, let's be honest. I think TV and those damn movies are the blame. When he was in Mexico, your mother didn't have no problem out of him, I think it is these United States and all its pro freedoms.

Look at the Black culture, it thrives on the image of being a gangster. I see this show called Miami Vice. You, seen this crap? It makes selling coke, a great thing to do. See TV? Damn TV? I will talk with him and set him straight about that kind of life.

The downfalls are everywhere in that life." "I think it best, if you did cousin. He looks up to you, Marcel, and I know why, but I don't care. If you can help me, I can help you. I will do the same with Junior. I will take him into my company and educate him while he is here."

Marcel Sr.'s voice had a grateful, glee in it. "Thank you, Oh, thank you, that would take the world off my shoulders. Now I want to talk shop. Are we free to speak?" "Sure, my dad said, as long as it is something legal." "Oh Michael, you are so funny. I have this house in Mexico City. I have been trying to get your mother to move in it, but she tells me that she is fine in her condo.

What I was thinking is that, you take the house off my hands and we will call it an even swap for the ninety-thousand. It's a three-level, split house. I bought it for thirty thousand. I will swap it for the money. I have turned it into a palace, with all marble, even the sinks and toilets. When DaVaughn comes back to Mexico, he can live there with your mother, plus your mother's house is too small.

When you all are in town, this will be perfect." "I agree. My mother does need a new house and you need the cash, so it works out fine." "I see the Patron in you Michael. I don't care what you say. I will start the paper work and it would best, if you just let me transfer it in your mother's name. I will have it all wrapped up in a week for you Michael.

Have DaVaughn pick me up tomorrow morning, so that I may talk with him before I leave to go back to Mexico. Do you think he will mind me talking to him about this problem?" "No, I think he will feel honored that you are taking an interest in him."

"He is a respectful boy. Michael, may I be frank with you? Your son is a natural leader and he could lead the clan now like a young prince would, but I know you do not approve of our life, we live in Mexico. I wish Junior had the smarts your boy has, the drive, the focus. The first time I met your boy, Michael, I felt in him, a Mexican heart. Your mother has done a great job with him.

He speaks Spanish. Think about it, a Black Spaniard! I can see how much he loves his Mexican family, especially my son. They hit it off from the first day. One day, I over heard him say to my son, how he loves the rancho, but how he wished, you were like me.

Michael, if what you tell me is true about the coca and him, then as soon as you can, send him back to Mexico where he was doing so good. I can keep him from such things at my rancho."

The whole time I was listening to Marcel and dad talk, I could only think, it was Mexico that taught me my new education in narco. Marcel was right though, I did one day want my own family and I wanted tobe a Patron, not a business man. The one thing I was sure of was that I wanted to be in the cartel.

I learned that in Mexico, a family runs different than in

America. I also realized in Mexico that the only way to have power is to have family who will do your bidding.

I believe in my heart that Mexico gave me a piece of culture, that I will die to protect, and that is, family is everything!

Chapter 9
WISH I WAS INNOCENT AGAIN

It seemed so funny to me, to see Cliff try to imitate Don Marcel. He was on the streets wearing cowboy hats and diamond belt buckles. My brother never even wore boots, but now he would say, "that is a boot, but these gators are art." It seemed to me that what he envisioned was happening for him, because I never saw him so happy as at this time in his life, right now. It was good to see him on such a high, that appeared as if, at any moment, he could float away.

I had a funny feeling about all this new found fame he was getting and it wasn't good. I learned how to hustle the old-fashioned way, hand to hand, as we called it. The street I use to live on was my brothers' and he wore his badge like a sheriff. I could see the slight changes in him. A mean streak was coming out slowly. My cousins were changing too. It seemed as if, they all took a big dose of ruthlessness and never put the bottle down.

This one street business would seem to most a little drop in the bucket in the whole scheme of the drug culture. Except, this little street business ran to the tune of one hundred thousand a month! I noticed that the drug world was nothing like on TV, where the people all say something witty and experience the fancy night life. We had money, yes, but we didn't change our way of living.

What is stated in this next sentence is the real truth for me... this was the beginning of the end of the simple life I was so use to. I wish so bad, that I was back in Mexico on the trails with Junior and I knew nothing of this new game I was involved in.

To me; Junior was better suited for this business, more than me, his dreams of this life, of money beyond money. One day I was sitting on the steps of our old house, when Antone, my cousin, pulled up. He and Cliff called each other cousin, so it made him my cousin too. "You busy?" he shouted out the car. "No." I walked toward the car, leaned in, and he said, "How many rocks do you have left before you can leave?" "Forty."

"Damn, you have not done shit this whole day." "Oh no, my cousin, I said, I had a hundred stones. Sixty times fifty a rock and you do the math. I had a great day. I just want to finish with an even stash." I could see he was impressed. "I want you to take a ride with me. "Why not, I said, I wasn't doing anything."

Now, let's just explain, who Antone is, in all this. He was Cliff's enforcer. He earned the name, "Beast" because he does what he wants, when he wants and he lives to prove one point in life: oppose him and you die! He takes no prisoners. On First Street, he killed over twenty people that I knew about. He really liked his job and Cliff loved him for it.

But I saw a second side to Antone, a jealous side to him. Ok, back to the ride. "Your brother is on the rise in this city. He is a ghetto star, but we all know, it's because you guys are half Mexican and that is on the real, he said sarcastically.

If I had family in the country where it all comes in at, I would have a connection too. I just laughed and said, (in Spanish)," but you don't and one day, I will have to kill you." I could tell he had no clue what I was saying, so I just said, it meant may one day you get your dream and chuckled. "Didn't Cliff, help you get this car?" "Yes, he did. He is a great guy, don't you think?"

"Yeah, your brother is a great guy. He is my favorite cousin." I could tell I made him feel uneasy, because he changed the subject fast. "I just needed you to ride with me, so I can run in this spot, deal with these cats I know, and roll out, but I need the car to stay double parked. I don't trust them at all. If you hear gun fire, just jump behind the wheel because I won't have time to drive and shoot, if I have too." "No problem, cousin." I had even brought my gun out today. I must have known, I might need it today. Just another day of, "what the hell am I doing with my life?"

We pulled up in front of this carry out. It seemed like any other, but I could tell something was different about this one. Then I spotted it. The place had no real doors. It had a bank-like glass, slot door. They served food like this, I thought. Genius!

Who would ever get a chance to catch you off guard? Antone got out and said, "Remember, shoot to kill." He went up to the window, said something to the guy inside, and then the window opened and a bag fell from it. He picked it up, then ran to the car. "Go, go, he said, I don't trust these guys. They give me the creeps, but they also are one of our best distributors.

Your brother tells us about Mexico. I hear the people are poor." "Poor people are everywhere, but the country does have its share of poor people. We also have a rich part that you will never find here. I miss it very much." "Cliff says that coke is everywhere down there.

That he has seen fields and fields of coke, is that true?" "Sure is, I said, but I never heard of the stuff, until Cliff bought it up. Rich people there are different from the rich here.

The father of a family is very important when the man is very rich; but it's funny, there, a grown man has to take orders like a child from the family Patron. Rich women live private lives from the public. You never see them. They live like rock stars here in the states.

The women are so beautiful, that they can have a man in the palm of their hands. One day, we will have to have you down Antone." "For sure. I want to see the coca fields." I never said anything to Cliff about the car ride, but let me tell you it was scary to me. The next day I woke up and started down to the block, when I was pulled over by two federal jump out units.

These are plain clothes head bashers that hide behind badges. The units are quite aggressive, if you ask me. I was surrounded by three cars. I felt important, due to all the attention they were causing by tying up the whole street for little old me.

One of the officers looked at me and then he yelled back to his partner, "It's him, what should we do?" He leaned in and took the keys and asked for my ID and registration. I gave him the ID my brother gave me. "You want me to believe you are twenty years old?

Shit boy, I got hair on my nuts that look older than you. Where did you get this ID? Who gave you this? Better yet, how the hell do you have a thirty-thousand-dollar car? Your brother is no fool. The car is in his name, I see."

"Yes, this is my brother's car. I'm just joy riding." At this time, his partner came to the window and said, "let's toss the car and see

What we can find. Get out boy and do it slowly, because I'm scared of drug dealers. They make me grab for my gun, you understand me? "Yes, Sir."

I looked down for a moment to collect myself and by the time I looked back up, the guns were out and at that time I knew I was involved in some serious shit. "You are Cliff's little brother?" "Yes, yes, I am sir." As I got out the car, I was told to sit on the curb of the street.

"DaVaughn is your name. We know who your whole family is. Tell me, how could such a straight guy like your dad have two criminals like you two, for sons? Go figure. Tell your brother, we are working hard to catch him and if we can't get him, you will do."

"Oh yeah, and tell him for me, (the other cop said), Don't die before I catch him. I have a score to settle with him." When he said that, my heart began to beat fast, because I could see the hate in his eyes.

He meant every word he said to me. "You got that boy? You can pick this car up from impound. Now get the hell out of here before I arrest you for being ugly. I ran to the pay phone on the corner and called Cliff. "Hey, they took the car, I screamed, and one cop said he wanted you not to die before he catches you.

I'm so shook, Cliff. They had guns in my face and everything."

"You need to calm down. Don't worry. We have a leak. I'm working on it, so just calm down. Catch a cab to dad's and I will see you later." "Ok, sure, Cliff, I mumbled. What about my car?" "Fuck that car. It's hot. Do you really want it back? I want you to go look for another 300 ZX.

It's a good car for you. Eric will meet you at dad's house. He will take you to look for a car. Trust me, you will have a car by the end of the day. Don't worry. Tell Eric to take you to Virginia, across Key bridge. Tell him to pay the whole thing in cash." "Ok." and I hung up the phone.

Eric was Antone's cousin on his father's side of the family. Eric was a mastermind at, shall we say, making problems go away. He was like an army solider. He never took his eye off the hustle. We use to call him "Professor" because he use to read books and sell drugs at the same time. He would hold class on the block. He taught me all about World War II.

He would say to me," knowledge is not in an institution. It's in the books they have in them so always read books. They give you knowledge." He taught me about the different key players in that war. He loved the Nazi party. I could never understand it because they hated everyone, I read.

He loved the man they called, Gerbil. He would tell me the key to taking things, is making the people think they should have them. Eric could manipulate people like Gerbil did for Germany. One day I was hanging with him, he bought this book called Mein Kofi out the house.

The author, for those who don't know, is Adolf Hitler.

Eric would always make quotes from this book. I would have to say he was a real deep fellow. His philosophy was very clear: "It's us and the world is our oyster."

"The police took your car? I hate when that happens especially, if it's a car you really like. I am glad you got your cherry bust though, now you can see that whenever the government wants something, it just takes it. We will have the same mentality when I'm done with our little group. I've had to ditch plenty of my cars or the police took them, so don't feel bad.

It happens to all of us. I had to burn a car once because I knew that they might have bugged it with that listening shit, so never take a car back from the police, my boy." "No problem, I said, after hearing that I won't ever take one back." "You are now in the middle of the game and you need to start acting and thinking like it.

Don't assume anything and never use the phone. I see great things in you. Like everyone else, I have to be honest, the money I am making now has helped me so much. My mother is very sick and we were having a hard time getting her medicines. They are so expensive, but now I can buy not just her meds, but I have her at Georgetown hospital.

I guess I would like to say from my heart, little cousin, if your family wasn't connected the way it is, I might have lost my mom and that is some real shit to me!

You will pass your brother in fame and power, but let me tell you, it's going to cost you something one day, that you would never have traded for all the power.

All great men pay this price. Remember it and also remember that he who wears the crown is forever alone. What made you come back from Mexico?" "This terrorist named, Mor Ma Kadifi started blowing up buildings around the American embassy in Mexico.

I mean a whole building comes down like a book of match stick bums. He killed over two hundred people in one building." "I would have come back too," Eric said. Let's discuss what kind of car we are looking for. Knowing your brother, he wants you to get something expensive.

I know just the car for you. I saw it last week. I was going to get it. It's your brother's favorite, a 1990, 300 ZX, champagne color with beige, leather seats. This car is hot! It even has rims on it and the windows are tinted."

We pulled in front of this dealer and a foreign guy came out treating me, like he knew me. "Is this the little guy who lost his car? Well, don't worry. I have something here that will suit you. Just look around.

"He wants the 300 ZX." "Are you sure that's not too much car for me? The feds are going to take that, just because it's so flashy." "Little cousin, don't worry. If they take it, we will just buy another. Trust me, we can afford it. Your brother is very rich, so let us worry about you." "Eric, do you know if I had this car in Mexico, that I would be so popular? Marcel and I would load it up with beer and go to all the outer towns and meet girls all day and all night.

Some of the most beautiful women are in some of the worse places. I miss that country so much. It sickens me to be here, now that I'm back, plus I miss my Grandmother.

Anyway, let's rap this up, I have to be home soon or my dad will blow his stack." Eric went in the building to hammer the deal. I walked around the back to see the car and I was in love with it. It was so flashy! It felt like it had special powers.

How stupid is that? I could feel this car was going to make me really happy. The salesman came out. "So, you are the proud owner? Do you know how much this car is? "No, I replied, who thinks about that?" I whipped back at him. I could see it irritated him, because he said, "Well, my friend, it must be nice to not have to know the price." "Yes, it is. Thank you. How long will it take to finish this?"

"You can go little man. Eric will do the paper work. Enjoy your new car." I jumped in the car and I felt like a rock star. I sped off like a bat out of hell, chirping the tires and screaming out the window to Eric standing in front of the lot. I came. I saw. I conquered.

I called Cliff when I got home. "Hey, I heard you got a great car. Where did you park it?" "I parked it in a private garage in one of the hotels around the corner." "Good thinking little brother because dad will kill you, if he sees you driving that car, so be careful.

Have you seen Don Marcel's house here? It is perfect for the next part of my plan. Expansion is the key." "Cliff, I want to go back to Mexico. I miss Grandmother, and I feel this is not for me.

Do you think I could take my car home?" "Sorry little brother, you can't take that home, but shit, just buy the damn thing again. We'll look into that. I'm sure there is one in Mexico somewhere." "Cliff, Eric made me laugh so hard. He thinks we are in the cartel.

He kept talking about the connection we have, Antone too. They all think we are like Don Marcel." "We are ignorant, and I am the Don." I laughed. "You a Don?" "Yeah, Don Marcel said he would support my dream, as long as I conduct business like they do.

He wants you and Junior back home, but there is a war going on. That is why Junior is staying with us. He is under your protection." "Well, I said sternly, I won't be here long. Trust me. I've heard stories about Don Marcel and the Delprado clan, but after seeing how much you are into this, I feel I need to stay and watch your back."

"Don't worry about me. I can handle myself little brother. You just focus on my money, you have tied up in the markets. How is it doing?" "It's doing well. Dad was right. This stock will make you rich. Oh, excuse me, richer." We both laughed.

"Is Junior really as ruthless as he seems?" "He wants me to really pull this off. He's excited about it. His dad is aware of his involvement. I had to tell because he asked, but he doesn't want him to know he knows, so keep it between us. Junior will be Don Marcel's collector. I will tell him, it's from dad and Junior will be none the wiser. His job is to just collect the money and your job is to move the money.

Who would think you would be carrying large sums of money? Now, let's go over, when you are carrying money. Always wear a suit and take taxi cabs, so if the feds ever get wind, you can say it was in the cab when you got in. Never carry a bag.

Use one of dad's old brief cases. Look like dad and no one will stop you." "Sure, no problem, but why did they buy a house here on 5th street?" "Don Marcel says he want to get his foot in the United States and he says he can see the potential in my business.

He is going to give me some help, if I give him forty percent of what I make. Do you understand what I am saying? He's going to help me take this city over and you will be my voice in Mexico. Don Marcel said I could use the house as a Trojan horse.

I can store all types of weapons there and when I go to war, I will already have my artillery in place. I can see why he is the Don of his family. He knows how to wage war like an army general. You should see him, DaVaughn.

He has maps of the whole city and has them marked with all types of shit going on. He has taken a liking to Eric and I don't like that, so I keep them apart.

Antone thinks that we should just fight until we are the last standing, but Eric reminds me of the third reich and how it fell due to fighting on all fronts. The difference between Antone and Eric is that Antone kills for the sport and Eric kills for glory.

What a mix to be in between." "Cliff, I said, I would not want to be in the middle of them." "Shit, DaVaughn, what the hell do you think, Don Marcel is in between? He really is in the hot seat with Antone loving his nick name, 'The Beast.'

Did you know he has a tattoo of that on his chest in big letters? Looks crazy to me, but he loves the fame he's getting from being so feared in the neighborhood. If it was up to the whole crew, we would kill everyone we saw who looked at one of us the wrong way."

"Cliff, I want to be honest with you about how I feel about this new business you are in. I like the money, love the fame and the lifestyle is great, but I have something cooking of my own. I need more money." "More money, he shouted, you have at least forty-thousand and you want more?

My little brother, a true business man! So, what's the thing? It's a stock I have been looking at and I know it will go up. I want to take a large position in this company.

Dad had me do a lot of research and this company will be the next IBM, trust me, I see it. I am using my money and Juniors' profits to start, but I still need more money, before I lose the window to buy the stock. Marcel and I have sixty thousand between the two of us. I need thirty-thousand more to make it a full even block of shares. I am trying to secure a thousand shares. It will work and I will make you a deal.

I will use the profits I earn to buy your way into the Delprado family. Let dad guide you Cliff. He can help your business become legit." "Legit? Hell no! I'm a gangster and you remember that little brother. I am the next to run this family. Do try to remember that when you talk to me, agreed?" "Yes, Cliff agreed.

DaVaughn, what is the name of this stock and should I include Don Marcel?" "The stock is Microsoft Computers and let me give you some good advice.

Cliff, never cross Don Marcel. He may treat us like family, but I have seen how he deals with his own family. No love, when you cross him." He's that cut throat, DaVaughn?"

"Cliff, he's worse. The men at the ranch who carry the guns, will do so until they die. Never to ever be more than just a hired gun. Junior said that most of the men came from the city after the government started cracking down on traffickers. He says that Don Marcel pays a thousand dollars for every kill they bring him.

Don Marcel is a heavy hitter for his town and Uncle is his advisor in this, so he must be just as ruthless. You should see Grandmother when she is at the rancho. Uncle treats her like she is still his little sister. It's funny.

She is so tough to us, but putty to them. I overheard Grandmother talking to him one day at the kitchen table about how the cartel has taken all the youth out of him. She also said that it was easier for the cartels, when they use to just steal cars and bring them across the border instead, of all the killings they do now. She makes such a fuss over him. He is a big deal in her life.

I believe he is a killer too. Junior also told me that Uncle gives him advice like, never fear death. It is just the end, coming for you. It spooked me when he said it. But I will end with this big brother, trust no one and deal swiftly. I got that from Don Marcel. Call you in the morning. Have to get to dads for dinner. See ya, bye homey.

Chapter 10

ONLY IF YOU ARE A CARTEL MEMBER

Don Marcel wanted me to take him to the airport. I found it odd, but you don't refuse him. I arrived at the hotel he was staying at which was the Plaza Hotel, a place that would cater to his every need. I thought if I traveled, I would only stay in this type of hotel.

I walked to the door of his room, took a deep breath, and knocked on the door. I heard him yell, "Enter." I turned the door handle and walked in. "It's me Patron, DaVaughn."

"Please come in my boy. I am not ready to go, so I will be in no hurry. Sit down. I want to discuss your life with you. We have never spoken on this level, but I feel it is time for me to do so with you. I thought, great, another lecture. That's all I need, early in the morning.

I just smiled and said, "I would be honored, Senior."

"Your father has told me of your little run in with the law. Let us speak plainly. My English is not so good, so excuse me. We are men, so let's talk like men and if at any time you have a question, please have no fear to ask me. Agreed?

I felt in you DaVaughn, a certain quality. Your father told me about you, your brother, and your cousin. I was so proud to hear you guys were trying to run your own business. Your father also said that you are the one with the brains and he said that I should be worried about your brother. He is a greedy man. Do not take offense. I just want you to be clear about what I know.

The path you have chosen is a hard one and you either go to prison for life or you are killed by someone close to you, so understand what you are choosing. I can see the Mexican culture in you and in this country that is a virtuous quality. You are a smart man and you are a thinker. Being a thinker in this country is good, but in Mexico, the Patron thinks on your behalf.

Do you understand what I mean by this?"

"Yes, I uttered, I understand." My hand kept jittering. I was very nervous and I kept sweating. "I'm sure your brother has told you I bought a house here. You and Junior are to live there. I am making you his bodyguard.

You will make sure he stays out of trouble and you will protect him with your life. In return for such a service, I will look after your Grandmother like she is my own mother, for you. I know how close you are to her. This honor I give to you might be the very key to the brass ring.

For you to be a body guard of a Patron is an honor and Junior will be the next Patron, so you have just been given a seat in my family. It means no one can touch you and not have to deal with me.

I give you the family name of Achoa." "May I speak Patron?" I am flattered at the honor of guarding Junior. I am also happy to know I am a member of the Delprado Cartel. Me, a cartel member!

I am a Black man who made it into the cartel. What an honor I feel today! Please do not tell Cliff. He will try to use me to leverage you or to ask for things on his behalf and I don't need the headache." He agreed.

"I also want you to tell Junior, I am his new guard. I will need one more thing Patron. I will need a number I can call at anytime to make sure I am making the right decisions when it comes to Junior's safety."

"This is what I mean DaVaughn, you are a thinker. I will set it up that you will be able to get ahold of me at any time." "Ok, you do know I have never killed anyone, Patron?" "Never DaVaughn? You will one day and that is when you will see the real beast in the world at play. Are there any other questions?" "No Sir, I am clear on my duty to you."

And with that said, he said, "I am glad to have you in my family now and he gaveme a kiss on the cheek and a strong embrace. Then he looked in my eyes with a stern look, "Never fail me, you understand?" "Yes, I understand."

On the way to the airport, Marcel kept asking me all types of questions. "DaVaughn, he said, why do you love Mexico so much? What makes you love my country so?

Most people visit, but they say they could never live there and here we have you, an American who hates to leave my country." "I love the fact, Sir, that men like you rule the provinces and have enough power to influence the government.

My Grandmother said that there was a time when the cartel could flat out tell the government, "No." "The Mexican government is weak now, but they are getting strong and we the cartel will have to either go to war with the government or we will strike a deal.

The United States is putting pressure on the government to track down and kill men like me, DaVaughn. The district attorney wants to be a judge and the judge wants to be part of Parliament and Parliament members want to be candidates for the presidency. These government positions are paid for by different cartel families trying to gain position in the government.

We hold elections for the people, but we the cartel make the decision of who gets what office. In Mexico, DaVaughn, you can kill politicians. But in the States, it is an open warrant for death. Your country has no mercy for such acts. Everyone has a Patron in Mexico. Even the president must answer to someone. You do what the cartel says or you die, is how we deal with our politicians. You now live under the same rules. You do as I say with no question or you die." When Marcel Sr. said this to me, every hair on the back of my neck stood up and I will never forget those words.

"When you return to me in Mexico, you will get a job and a list of duties. Your duty, I can see, will be to look after your Patron. Junior, my son is your Patron. Understand?" "Yes, I do. I won't let you down, Patron." "I know you won't." I could see the seriousness in his face. I was so glad the airport exit was coming up. "You know, DaVaughn, I will never visit this country again. It isn't safe for me."

We pulled in front of the airport and I got out and got his bags. We looked at each other with a smile, but only my smile was a polite grin that hid the fear I was feeling. "Now remember, he said, Junior is in your hands." I know it is a big request of your Patron, but I have faith in you, my little man. If you need help, just call and I will send it.

If you and Junior ever get in hot water, head to El Paso, Texas.

I have guards there and my brother is the Patron of Juarez. Just get my son there and protection will be waiting for you." "You know, he has a temper, Patron." "Yes, I know, but he's your cousin and he will listen to you. I have made it very clear to him that he is to listen and to stay out of trouble.

Now I must go. Take this money. I won't need this. You guys go have a good time with it." I looked at the money at a quick glance and saw it was about five thousand there.

"I love you DaVaughn." "I love you too, Patron." I kissed his hand as to respect his position and he disappeared in the airport. That was a ride I will never forget.

Now that I have been given this duty, I find myself wondering why does Junior need a bodyguard?

It would not take long for me to find out. It was at a party in Adams Morgan, the Northwest part of town. It was a real Latin place in the city. Junior told me he knew where some midlevel cartel members meet. He said we should go meet some of the other members. I thought sure, why not. Who doesn't want to meet the "in" crowd?

We pulled up in front of this house that was barred from the ground up. You had to enter it from the alley. It had a steel door with a slot in it. A guy opened the slot. Junior gave him a name and the door opened.

The whole house was transformed to look like a western lounge. It looked like something you would see on the outskirts of Mexico. I was impressed. You would never have figured such a place was inside this dump. It wasn't big, but it was three levels of salsa music and all the drinks you want.

There were rooms that were set up like brothel beds and the

best thing of all, it was all free! There had to be at least thirty people in this house. We walked up to the upper levels and it got better with each floor. So many naked women, all ready to do what you pay them for.

Junior said to me, "I hear they have a cartel members' only room. We should be in there." We walked to the last level where there was a guy standing in front of a staircase. The man asked, "Are you a mule or a member?" Junior said, "I am a member. I am Marcel Delprados's son and that should be enough for you. He gave the guy a hundred-dollar bill and we walked up the stairs.

"Junior, what the hell is a mule?" "It's a donkey." "I know. But what the hell was he talking about?" Junior burst out laughing. "You idiot, he said, a mule is someone who brings the coca across the border. Now this is the level of life. All men should live on salsa blasting, women in cages, and men dressed in western gear." It looked like the perfect picture. Junior and I took a seat behind these young guys.

They had to be in their late twenties. I heard one of them say, "I hear there is a Delprado among us. "I knew we were in for trouble and we had not been in the place an hour yet. Fuck you! If I heard him say it, then I knew Junior did. So here we go. "I am a Delprado," Junior said. The look on their faces was as cold as ice.

One of the guys leaned over and said, "So you belong to that murderous family? I use to live in your town and I have seen how your family rose to the top on the backs of good people. My brother was killed by your family. I can remember when your family was nothing more than car thieves. Now your family runs the Plaza."

Junior stood up and pulled out a small hand gun and he didn't stop pulling the trigger until he could only hear the click of the empty magazine. It all happen so fast. People were running everywhere! The guy was in mid-sentence when Junior shot him. I grabbed Junior.

"Do you have any more bullets?" he said.

"I have an extra clip in my sock and this is what we are going to do. I'm going to shoot our way out of here, so stand behind me, don't let go, and whatever you do, don't stop running."

To our surprise, the place was clear and most of the people left were the strippers and the bartender. We got to the second level and there was nothing. This was too good to be true and it was.

We ran out the side door opposite to the one we came in and something told me that's where they would expect us to go, but I shot the glass out the side door and we both came crashing through. I don't think we even hit the ground. We just kept running. We were close to Rock Creek Park and I knew this park like the back of my hand. I yelled, "Come on Marcel. Fuck the car.

We have to go." I took a side street, jumped a fence, and we were in the park. I told Junior to keep up. We had to get the hell out of there. We ran for about a mile, then slowed up to a walk. "I'm sorry, Primo," Junior said gasping for breath. Give me a minute. I feel like I'm going to be sick. That guy had no right to speak to me like that. He was a real asshole, but I guess he won't be shooting his mouth off any more." He started to laugh. "Woo baby, he said, you were great!

I was totally stumped on how you knew to go out the window?" I said, everybody knows that's where the bad guy waits for you and I started to laugh. Now let's get home." We started to walk when Junior said, "I am in debt to you. You risked your life for me and I am proud of you. Thank you, brother!" I could tell it wasn't bullshit. He really meant it. I have never killed before, but I am glad I did. No one disrespects the Delprado name and lives.

When we got back home to Junior's house, I called Cliff and told him what happened. But this dumb ass wasn't any help. He just said, "way to go and next time, take more men with you." I thought, thanks for nothing and hung up the phone.

"I got some mota," Junior said. "What the hell is mota?" "You Americans call it weed. Smoke with me. It will calm you down." I took one puff and I was on cloud nine. "Where did you find this? I've had dope before, but nothing this strong." "I got it from this Columbian chick I've been screwing." "This is some strong shit here. We have to get you out of here.

The police will start looking for you. There were too many witnesses. We have to pack you up tonight and you need to be on your way to El Paso. I have to make a call." I called the rancho in Mexico. "Hello, Uncle is that you?" "Yes, it is me, son. What's wrong?"

"I have to get Junior to El Paso like now, or the law will catch him here." I could hear my Uncle spring up. "I'll send someone for you both. Where are you?" "We at the house." "Stay there. I will have someone on their way to you. Tell Junior to not travel with any of the stuff. Tell him to leave everything and you make sure he doesn't have any coca on him. "Yes, I understand."

Here again, the ball is thrown in my lap. Junior went into the master bedroom and came back with a bag full of coca. "How much is this?" "It's six kilos of this stuff called crack. Your brother has shown me how to make the powder turn into a hard form and it doesn't use a lot of the coca to make the product.

He said one kilo of raw coca can make three kilos of crack, so I asked Uncle to send me some raw product and this is what I made. Your brother can help you get rid of this stuff. But I have a sad feeling, because here is the money I have made.

I know I have to leave it here with you, so I guess today is your lucky day. It's fifty-thousand in this bag. Just invest it in something and tell me about it." We both chuckled. "You bet. I will as soon as I get back home.

Why can't you take it with you? I don't understand." "Because if I'm caught with it, the officials will hold me ransom for more stuff. You would think this would be enough for anyone, but nope they will want more. Then they will have to kill me, so I don't tell. So, you see?" "Fuck this shit. It's not worth my life." We had gone from, no money to swimming in it.

"My cousin, I pray that you don't get in trouble over last night. Do you think they will come for you?" I said, "Let's see, a ton of witnesses, my car left there, and on top of that, my brother is wanted by the police. I'd say they will come for me. Damn, I just can't catch a break. I have to get back to Mexico." I packed up the stuff and called a limo service.

With this type of cash and dope, I could not trust it to a cab ride. Why not take a limo? I have the money to do so. "I wish I could take that limo ride with you, DaVaughn." I waited with Junior all morning for his ride to come. Two men in a black Mercedez pulled in front of the house. One of the men stood at the car while the other got Juniors' bags. "Well, I said to Junior, it seems we will be apart again for a while, but I will make it home.

Trust me and I will do right with the other thing. Trust me." The man came back out the house with Juniors' bag. He looked at Junior and said, "There is nothing in this bag I should hide, is there?"

"No, Junior said, unless you want me to hide it in my socks." Then he just started laughing.

Unfortunately, the man did not see the humor in the joke and just headed to the car. I gave Marcel a kiss on both cheeks and then his hand. "I will not fail you."

"I know, Cousin, and I won't fail you. See you in Mexico." Then Junior walked to the car and got in. I found it bizarre that one of the men sat in the back with Junior. Then it came to me. He is his shield now.

I took one last look and then I waited on the steps for my ride. I waited for about forty minutes and then the limo pulled up. I could not help but wonder, what would the Patron do to Junior?

The driver stepped out the car, "Mr. Kidd?" It sounded good when he said it. "Do you have any other bags?"

"No, I just have this one duffle bag and I will handle this. Thank you." He opened up the door and I got in. I sat back in the seat and just blurted out my father's West Virginia address. "You know that's two hours away?"

"Yes, I know. I have the money to pay for it. Here is two-hundred for you and five-hundred for the ride. Please don't drive fast. I'm in no hurry."

I was going to the cabin because as a boy, my dad would hunt with us and he would say if you want to keep your clothes dry, bury them in a hollow tree. So, I thought I would bury the stuff and take some time to figure things out. My father kept this cabin, so he could hold private meetings there. It was a very secluded place.

It amazes me that people don't realize that just 2 hours from

D.C., mountains exist. West Virginia is a beautiful place. It has a feeling of frontier living. I asked the driver to put the window up and that I had to make a call, so I would like some privacy.

The shield between us went up and I picked up the phone. I called my Dad. The phone rang twice, then I heard 'good evening' in his business voice. "Dad, it's me. I'm in trouble. Junior is on his way back to Mexico. Don Marcel has him. I'm on my way to the cabin.

I am going to stay there, if that is ok?" "Son, how bad is it? A detective came by and said that your car was implicated in a murder. Please say, it's not so." My silence said it all to him.

"Don't answer any questions. Call this number from Pennsylvania and let my lawyer deal with it. I will let you know when to come back, so go to the cabin. I will send for you when it seems clear. I love you, boy." "I know, I know, Dad. Will you call Cliff and tell him dad?" "No, DaVaughn. I will not tell him. You know your brothers' phone may have ears."

Afterwards, I then called the rancho in Mexico. "Hello." (in Spanish, I heard). I could tell from the voice, it was the Patron. "It's me, Sir."

"DaVaughn, my little angel, he said, my son tells me great things of you. He told me what happened.

I want to thank you for doing such a good job. What can I do for you? Are you safe? You can come here too, but you may never be able to go back?"

"Sir, I just wanted to apologize for failing you." "Oh, my boy, you did not fail me. What do you think? That the guards did a better job? You risked your life for your family. I commend you boy. Junior told me what he left you. Let's use this as my first gift to you." "I can have it all?"

He said, it's all yours." I even have a bit of good news. Your Grandmother moved in the house finally, and she has made some new friends. She loves it.

I will have Junior look after her till you return. It's the least he can do." "Thank you, Patron. I really thank you."

"DaVaughn, he said, I want you to do me a favor. Your brother is becoming a little known and I hear he is under investigation. That isn't good. It could ruin everything.

You talk to him for me and tell him, I want him to think about coming here for a while. It's time.

The phone is getting ready to go out, so I will say this, "Do what you have to do to get back to me." Then the phone went dead.

As the car drove further and further into the mountains, I felt a burden lift off of me. We crossed into West Virginia and I told the driver to stop somewhere so I can get some food. We arrived in front of the cabin.

The cabin sat on10 acres, so the house sat back in the woods. It was five o'clock and it was starting to get dark. I went around back and dug in the tree where we hide the spare key. I opened the door and flicked on the lights. No power! Shit. Then I remembered my dad always shuts the power off from the main box. I went to the garage and threw the switch and the lights came on.

I hadn't been here in years and it looked better than I remembered. It had three bedrooms, a loft and was da shit in fashion. It reminded me of a French parlor. I should have just bought Junior here.

I'm seventeen years old now and life is moving fast for me. I sat down to clear my head in my dad's favorite chair and smoked some herb I had brought with me. There was this painting that kept grabbing my attention on the wall. It was a painting of Napoleon at the battle of Water Loo.

I thought about how Napoleon must have felt to be defeated after doing so much. Maybe I am like him, starting fast to die slowly. Then I gazed at the bag with my new wealth. It could be worst. I have at least two hundred in coke and about seventy-five thousand in cash, plus my investments. Like I said, it could be worse.

Chapter 11
THE REIGN OF TERROR

I named this chapter The Reign of Terror and I think after you read this, you will agree. Cliff and Eric decided it was time to take more of the city for their own. Most people think I mean take a major piece of territory. No, they wanted an extra five streets in all directions for their own. Cliff wanted to expand and he wanted to make a statement to the city that the First Street crew was not to be taken lightly. Eric informed me that Cliff is the one pushing this war.

"We don't really care," Eric told me. My brother had a private objective though. He had a beef with a Crew in the North East side of town. The Montana crew was a small click of guys who believed in death to all who made a mistake and came down their street. Cliff told me that this crew was cutting into his piece of the pie because they had more distributors than he did.

He knew if he got rid of them, all those needy distributors would need jobs and it would mean more money for him. No need to kill the whole snake, he would say. All you have to do is just cut off the head and the body will follow.

It was three months into my disappearing act, when I got a call from Cliff.

He said that he knew I was on vacation, but we have a business to run. I need your help with a little something. I will meet you in Hagerstown, Maryland. I need you to leave now. I'm leaving out the door and I'll be on exit forty.

Just keep a look out." "Ok, I said, I know how to keep a low profile or the man will come see you. Just fit in. Don't stick out. They still have KKK in these hills and they meet and rant about white power.

It is known that a Black man doesn't want to find himself on a dark road with them at night. "Ok, see you then." When we met at the exit, there was a change of plans. All we did was come back to the cabin with some of the cousins following us.

We all entered the cabin at the same time. Everyone took a seat around the room. Cliff said, "Ok, I called this meeting." Antone stuck his hand in the air. Yes, Antone?" "One: Great place! Two: Are we staying the whole weekend or is this another of your thirty-day gangster seminars?"

We all laughed at what Antone said, but I could see that Cliff was in no joking mood. "If you give me a chance, Antone, I will explain everything. Let's first have a drink and talk about where we are in this war we started." Everyone shook their heads. "I even did you all a favor.

I called this girl up and she is bringing a chick for each of us. So, how's that for a seminar. I even got something for you little brother. I hear she is beautiful like the women in Mexico. I bought beer and champagne.

There is a bottle for each of you and take a look at this herb I found. I bought a pound for just us to smoke up and for those who like a little more, here is some of Mexico's finest product. It will be in the kitchen, just in case, we were followed.

We wouldn't want to get caught with coke on the table, now would we? Eric leaned over and whispered to me, "You didn't know Cliff liked the powder, did you?" "No, I didn't, I said. How long has this been going on?"

"It's been on and off for the last two years." "Huh? I will deal with this.

If Don Marcel hears about this, it's curtains for all of us. He hates men who use the product. He always says, the man who likes to get high will one day stop making money, because the drug becomes more important." We were interrupted by Cliff. "Excuse me, you two? Would you like to share your private convo?" "No, go ahead." "Thank you.

Now, as I was saying. I have entertainment for us. I bought this movie I heard about. It's about this guy in Miami who makes a lot of money in the coke business. The name of the movie is Scar Face. So, everyone please go do their thing and I will see you guys at dinner."

Then he looked at me and said, "I want to talk to you on the balcony." I said, "Now?" "Yes, do you know a better time?" I could tell, I pissed him off.

We stepped outside away from any ears. "Little brother, I need you more than ever now. I am going to make you a delivery boy for me. I know it is a crappy job, but I can't let the cops see us all together and my phones are bugged.

You will deliver our messages for us to each other. This will be the last time we all meet together, so I made up a code for us like the navy does. Only you can deliver a message.

This will keep the cops guessing. Have a good time this weekend because things are going to change. I have bought pagers for us and I will only use numbers to spell my messages out to you. You will then deliver it to whom it's addressed to.

"Sure, Cliff, I'll do anything for you." "Little brother, I saw that in a movie. The Army was using that technique so the Germans would not know their plan." "Cliff, are you Ok?"

"Sure, my brother. But I have to say this, war is taking its toll on me. I have turned the city upside down. Oh yeah, Junior has a warrant for his arrest. They found the gun, but they have no fingerprints. They came by Dad's office looking for him, I heard. The car, well, they are trying to link it to the crime, but they can't, because I had the car reported stolen and it's not in your name.

It looks like Junior stole the car. It keeps you out of the picture. The only bad news is that they are holding your car and

You know the rules, it's no good when it's been in their hands. You can't keep a car, can you?" We both laughed.

"No, it seems the feds want me to walk. It's Ok though, because I want to tell you something. I am not made for this life. I will help you, but I want to stay in the background, Ok. I want to be more than just a violent killer. I want to be known as an author. I am going to write a book one day about our family."

"What are you going to write about, how a Black Mexican family found its way into the Mexican cartel? Shit, that does sound like a great story. Just make sure you give me my due. We are in the first phase of success, but after all is said and done, we will be rich beyond our dreams. I see it like this DaVaughn, we will either be rich or dead, so what's there to worry about?"

When Cliff said I might be dead, my heart felt a sharp pain. I could not fathom the thought of dying so young, so I just nodded my head and said, "We won't lose. You are the best of the best and I believe in you.

You are the Domo and I know you will make our family proud. I didn't tell you this, but before Don Marcel made me Juniors' body guard, he said I was part of the Delprado family.

"Are you trying to tell me what I think DaVaughn?" "Yea, I'm in the cartel under the Delprados. Don Marcel said that I could ask for support and I'm going to ask him to send some real killers to help you out."

"So, you're in the cartel? How the fuck did you get in and I didn't? Well, your gain is my gain. This changes everything. Ask the Domo, if he will send me two men that are skilled in torture, that can speak English, and are loyal to him.

Tell him, I also need weapons. My little brother, again, you prove to be the best brother a man could ask for. You little shit! Oh, I'm sorry DaVaughn. I still can't believe it. You in the cartel!" He threw his arm over my shoulder and we went back inside.

When we walked in, I could hardly see. The room was full of smoke and the table looked like someone was baking a cake. It was coke all over it. I sat next to Antone and he said, "Hey, Amigo, try this. It is some of the best herb I have ever had. I took a puff of the cigar wrapped herb and started choking. I felt great though.

"Here, you can have it. I'm high enough. Have you seen the girls? They are here and yours is fine, buddy. Your brother hooked you up. Here they come now." They all came from upstairs. One by one, the room filled with one pretty woman after another. "Which one is mine, Antone?" "Here she comes now."

"Hello, she said, are you DaVaughn?" "Yea, I'm him." "I've been looking for you. My name is Valarie, your date for the weekend. Do you mind if I smoke that with you? She grabbed the cigar and then she sat down on my lap. I'm not shy. I like to be me and me right now is digging you. You are so young. I hope I don't get in trouble." We both laughed.

"Cliff is your brother, right?" "Yes, he's my brother." I met him once at a club in town. He is a nice guy. Do you mind if I ask, how old you are?" "Eighteen." "Really? You don't look it at all. You look like you are about twenty-one. I am twenty-eight." "She was so beautiful." She looked like she was Indian or somewhere from the middle east. Her hair was in two braids and it was so long, it stretched pass her ass.

She had skin like almond cream and she was a little shorter than me, considering I'm only five feet, five inches. She was a mini bite, but she had an ass that was shaped like an onion! It was so plump.

"Have you seen our room?" "Yes, I set this all up." "You have nice taste. You seem to be a great guy, but you are so young. I feel a little strange, but at the same time, I want to be with you tonight so let's just take it slow. With that she smiled and said, "So Mister, what would you like for me to cook you tonight? I'm a very good cook.

You go take a shower and I will cook you something and bring it up to you." After we ate, we laid on the bed and talked about the world. Then it was like I said something she wanted to hear because she stood up and started to undress. "Here is your dessert," she said. And it was on!

The first night in the cabin was the best for me. I awoke early the next morning before everyone, so I could practice what I would say, if Cliff asked me any questions. We all went for a walk down the creek. It was about ten in the morning.

We all took seats around this big rock. Cliff climbed to the top and took a seat. "I have asked you all here to discuss our futures and how they will change. We have had a good run making this little table scrap money, but I feel we need a bigger territory.

I feel we can now expand further outside the city limits of Maryland and Virginia.

I hear Spring break is a gold mine. I want to plant a flag in every major city in this cursed country.

I feel that if we put our brains together, we can win this war we are now in. Northeast is small potatoes. Don't worry. I'm doing things you don't see. If we put them out of business, it will have a domino effect and other crews will fold to our will. This war is good for two reasons.

One reason is that, with them out of the way, our profits will soar. The second reason is, it gives time to see who can really cut it in this type of life. I have compiled a list of their top crew members and top money makers.

I plan to run them all in the ground before the end of the year with your help. It's very simple. I need each of you to choose a name and that name is your target. I want each of you to know that you must finish your task or at the end of this, I will finish you off myself for being the weak link. If any of you should finish their task early, then you must help with the other tasks.

We are a family, Yes? The plan is full proof. When the money stops for them, then we send in the Latins to throw them off our scent. I will confuse the top players around there. They will think the Latins are trying to take over. I also want you to pick a family member of your target for leverage, if you miss your target.

I want the message to get across that if you don't move, we will move your family permanently. My Uncle in Mexico supports us and he wants us to plan to be successful. I know it is risky, but together we will run that city."

Before he could finish talking, Eric stood up. "What is the reward for each of us, if we do go along with you?" "If you give me a minute, I will get to all of that.

I hope you complete your task as fast as you open your mouth at the wrong time. Now sit down and don't ask me questions like that, because it implies, I haven't thought this through.

Now, before I was so rudely interrupted, who wants out? Let's get to that delicate matter because if you are in, then it will be to the death. Anyone who isn't with us, please get the fuck out now. I have thought this through and I feel that if anyone should abandon his duty to the clan, then he should be made a target.

I am putting fifty-thousand up for the head of any trader and I mean that exactly the way I said it. I want his head cut off and bought to me, family or not family, to me. The rules apply for all the same. I think this is fair. It will keep us all focused. I am going to make my little brother, our messenger.

He will be the only one that will be calling you or meeting with you. This way, the cops won't get us all together or tape our conversations. Do you all agree?" One by one, they all did. "It will also help, because he is young.

They would never think he would be the mouth between us. Now, let's talk strategy and weapons. I have taken the liberty to hire a skilled deer hunter to show you how to cut a corpse up into pieces, except we will be using deer for practice. He is also going to show each of you how to use a rifle with a scope and a hunting bow."

Antone said, "Damn, you are going to turn us into the Army." "You will be when I'm done with you. Now, if you are in, let me hear you." Everyone was so pumped. We all screamed, "Cliff, Cliff, Cliff."

"Ok, my friends, one more thing, I don't want a lot of bodies on the streets, so you must not have cowboy shoot outs. We will take a crash course in hunting and disposal. You should study your prey, then you can hunt them.

I will allow funds for certain weapons from the war chest. Each member will start off with the same number of weapons and will be given more as needed. Each member will receive a duffle bag with the following: four one hundred milligram syringes for injections, two hunting rifles with scopes, a hunting bow with arrows, four twenty-two caliber hand guns with potato silencers, two combat knives, two cattle prod shockers, and four pair of hand cuffs.

I saved the best for last. I have 8 sticks of demolition TNT, but I will only use them as a last measure, because if you get to blowing up the city, every FBI agent will be gunning for us. All bodies must be brought to the mountains and destroyed and dismembered. You can all thank my Uncle for the weapons one day. I told you, he wants us to win. And we will or die trying!

Then it started. He pulled out a bag. "Here is the bag of names. Pick one. I don't want anyone to tell his or her target. I will just check the obituaries for their names." I raised my hand and said, "I will meet each of you in Mexico before the end of the year with a message from Cliff on what will be the next phase of his plan.

I'm sure you will all love it there. I think it is best this way, just in case one of us falls under investigation, we can just stay there until the war blows over. Let's say someone else falls, then he can help rescue them from the feds.

It's like a safety net. If you think the heat is on, head for Mexico. It gives us all a good alibi. I suggest you all get a fake ID because you don't want your name in the border log book and do not fly.

I will meet you in a border town and then transport you to Mexico. Airports keep records. I am under the Delprado protection, so they will help us from the Mexican side with whatever I may need to safely transport you to Mexico City, so don't worry."

The look on their faces seemed to be a cave man look. "You mean we will have to leave the country if we get hot? "Is this what you're saying?" Cliff stood up and answered, "I would think so or should we all go to jail?" "Eric, are you scared to leave this land, Antone asked?"

"No, I'm just wondering what the hell I would do in Mexico?" We all laughed. "Cliff, I think your little brother is after your job." "I would love it, but he wants to live near the cartel, not us little folks." "Ok, then gentlemen. Is there anything else?" We all answered, "No." So, it's agreed. We will push the fucks off the earth.

Good will, hunting men. You will receive your tools when you leave and as an added bonus, here is twenty-thousand for each of you. It is a gesture from my heart. I also have your code books. I will be changing these books every thirty days. So, don't get use to them. They will change all the time. I also have a paper for you all to sign. This is an insurance policy I put together for all of us.

It is to ensure that we will survive no matter the lost and that there is money to continue the war. If I am killed, then this group receives seventy-five thousand for me. With the whole policy all together, that would be eight-hundred thousand. But then, none of us is here to spend it." We all laughed ecstatically.

"I also have this other paper for you to sign. This is to include you all on the brokerage account. It's about thirty-thousand in there for trading purposes, stocks, and bonds. I hear these CD's are great for hiding money. My little brother says that West Virginia is the best place to hide, if it gets hot. Just pick a mountain and wait for us to come get you."

I stood up and explained my plan of escape. "My Uncle has purchased a fifty-acre plot. It is in the mountains, not too far from here. It's only one hour and thirty minutes from D.C., so it's not far from you. I will show all of you where I hid a camper. It will always have clothes, weapons, a laptop, and food. "You know, damn, enough for you to survive!

I even left books out there about hunting and medical attention. When you finish your task on the list, then go there and stay till the heat is off or till we come get you." "Little brother, you were made for this world. It's a deal.'" Cliff said. Then we all headed toward the cabin.

While we were walking, Cliff leaned over and whispered in my ear, "Uncle Marcel was right. You are a man that should be in the cartel. You have brains. Have you heard from Junior?" "No, but I have to talk to Don Marcel and he sends you his best.

He really thinks highly of you. The only reason I am in the Delprado family is because Junior needed a baby sitter." "You funny, little brother." "I try." We both laughed. "Just remember, Cliff, you are the Patron and he who does not listen to you in this group should die. "Remember that." "It's all I think about," he said, all I think about."

Chapter 12
PROTECTING YOUR FAMILIES FUTURE

A party you won't forget is the slogan that ran through my head. Eric arrived first in Mexico. I singled him out the whole crowd. He wasn't hard to find because he didn't have boots and a hat on. "Hey, I yelled, over here. How was your flight?"

"It was nice. The rest of the gang is behind me in flights. We all thought it best to take different planes. So, this is Mexico? It's hot as hell here. Let's get some air condition." "No problem. The car is this way. We can go sightseeing a little." I took him through the countryside. I told the driver we wanted to see the old-world parts of Mexico.

We ended up in this town West of the Gulf of Mexico, a small, little horse and buggy kind of town. I planned to stash each one of them in different parts of Mexico, so that way, their disappearances would come as no shock considering each town had a crime rate of a hundred percent. This way, the embassy won't link the murders together. My Uncle had given me this little bit of advice.

One by one, they all arrived that day and one by one, I stashed them around town. I told them it was for their protection. As I greeted each one with joy, I knew it would be the last time I would see any of them again after this trip.

On the day of my party, I took them into Mexico City to see the city. We drank and smoked so much weed that day. I was so high, but I wasn't so high that it would affect my decision to get rid of all of them. Junior and I planned it like this.

We would take them by surprise. We would stage a phony argument between one of the ranch hands and one of the maids from the house. But let me tell you, Sophia is no average maid. She is so pretty that men throw money at her when she walked through the town.

We planned it to take place in the big arena where the bull fights take place and where the upper cartel members gather for social meetings with the average man. Our plan was that the ranch hand would play the role of a cartel member of high status.

Since everyone knew Junior, it was easy to believe he would be in the company of such men. Sophia was told to flirt with Eric with her eyes and to get his attention by showing him the inside of her skirt. We made sure we could all see though, believe me!

She would give him her number and ask for his. When we get back to the house, it would be discovered by one of the guards who checked you as you go in the party. We made sure the guy she was supposed to be with, just so happened to be the guy behind Eric. He would see the number and become insulted. Then I would spring my trap. I would murder each one on the way back to the hotel.

My Uncle even gave me some help. He gave me one of his best shooters. As usual, Junior played the part of a trafficker. He arrived on cue in rare performance, dressed in his best boots and hat. His belt buckle had so many diamonds in it, it would blind you when you glared at it. And the most important piece of a traffickers' wardrobe is their bodyguards. Marcel was surrounded by at least ten men.

When they came in the arena, you could see the people move out of his way. Eric tapped me on the shoulder and asked, "Is that Junior? Damn, he sure is up the ladder, huh?" "Yep, number two in the line." Junior sent four of his guards to fetch me. "Excuse me fellows, I must go pay my respects. I'll be right back." As I walked away, I could see that they knew this was the real deal in this country.

I walked up to Junior and kissed his hand. "Cousin, you are so dramatic, but someone could take lessons from you. Ha! Is Sophia here?" "Yes." "Good, I want her to ask him a lot of questions, so he will be taken with her. Tell her to just flirt with her body and he will do the rest.

Americans are so arrogant, he will think she really wants him. I motioned over to Eric and the rest to come join us. Even though Eric had met Junior before, he seemed a little nervous to shake his hand. Junior later told me his hand was wet and shaky. They look like fish out of water and for once, I was the shark.

"Let us go sit down, Junior said, in my fathers' box seats." When we sat down, we took up the whole row of seats. Some people even moved out of respect for the Delprado family. Sophia sat next to Eric and she kept fidgeting with her dress. The split on it ran all the way up her thigh. We all had a hard time concentrating.

"Hey Eric, Junior said, I hear you are like me, you like green tobacco." "Yeah, I do. Do you know where I can get some?" "My men will escort you. Sophia asked Junior, would he mind if she went too because she needed to use the ladies' room. "Sure, why not?" Eric later told me she was hot for him. He stated this on the way to the bathroom, and that she kissed him. He was so happy when I think back. He said, it went like this:

"So, you are from the Americas?" "Yeah, I'm American." "I want to live there one day. Would you take me there if you could?" "I wouldn't just take you, you could ride on my back." And they both laughed. "You are very beautiful, but I guess you know that. Do you smoke weed or green tobacco?" She smiled and said, "All the time. You can get as much as you want from that guy over there. I will go with you. Tell the guards we are Ok and to wait here. I know we don't know each other, but I want to get to know you while you are in Mexico. Maybe I could show you around." He said, she licked her lips as to imply something more was on her mind.

When Eric came back to his seat with a smile of ecstasy, I smiled. "By the smile on your face, I take it, you found some good green?" "Oh, I found something just as good. I found great green." We all laughed. I could tell he fell for the trap.

The bull fights went on and Junior started to become restless. "Hey, we can leave, whenever you are ready, Junior. Let's go to the ranch for a swim in the river. Junior leaned over to my ear and said, "Uncle is not ready for us yet, so we have to waste some more time. "I just want to see the next bull, then we can go." He said that out loud so that the others could hear.

Two hours went by before the phone rang. It was Uncle. "Tell DaVaughn to inform his friends that we searched at the house for weapons and that if they want to hide something personal, it's best if they put it in their shoe. But it was a trick, so that way, we won't have to take a lot of time looking for the number.

We started up to the house. Junior asked Eric to ride in his car with him and Antone seemed to be a little jealous, so even this part was working in my plan. How predictable people can be. I calmed him down by assuring him. "Trust me, Antone, you don't want to ride in there. Junior gets shot at least twice a week. You are safer in this car with me."

We finally got to the house and my Uncle had all the ranch hands in front of the main house to show the Delprado Army. "I will need you all to enter the house single file and you all have to be checked for weapons. It won't take long. Just comply and it all will move smoothly.

DaVaughn, you and your friends can go first." The front lobby was set up like a court house entrance one way in, one way out, and guards everywhere.

We all got in line and I went first, then Eric, then Antone.

As I was going in, I heard, of course, when Eric took off his shoe and the guard started banging them together until, (you guessed it), the phone number fell from the shoe. The ranch hand behind him became infuriated accusing Eric of trying to take his woman. Uncle came to the front of us. "What is this about?"

"Sir, this man has my woman's telephone number stuffed in his shoe. I will not stand for such disrespect. I am a member of the Ochoa cartel and this is a slap in the face from you Delprados." Junior then got involved. He ran up to me and grabbed me by the collar. "These are your friends'. This is what you bring to my house?

No one disrespects a guess of mine. No one, you got that? I suggest you take your cousin to the airport tomorrow because if I am asked for his life, then it will be granted." Junior put his hand in the air to motion for support and boy did he get it.

Eric was surrounded. Then Junior walked up to him and said, "You have cost me and no one cost me. If I find you in Mexico tomorrow by sundown, I'm killing you personally." Then with a wave of his hand, he motioned them to escort us out to the car.

My uncle was a perfect actor. "You have done a major thing young man. This country is not
like the United States. Men live by honor here. This is what we will do, I will hide you because I know that guy and when he gets the drink in him, he will want revenge.

You must leave Mexico tomorrow, all of you, for your own good. I will have the driver take you all back to your hotels. He will take you one at a time, that way it will give you time to apologize to Junior" We all agreed.

Eric said, "I must say, I'm very sorry for my deed." "No, you should leave first son. I think it best. It would be best for you all. The rest of you should come sit at my table, that way no disrespect will come to you."

One by one, the driver came and left and with each return, I knew one was dead. When the car finally came back the third time for Antone, my stomach felt a little bubbly.

He, to me, was a true gangster and I felt like he could read your mind. But I knew I had to be strong for Cliff's sake. I knew that once the war was over, he was going to kill Cliff.

As Antone got in the car, I waved, and said "All will be well, I will make the arrangements for you guys to leave
tomorrow." He nodded Ok and he got in the car. "Uncle, I am so sorry to have to had asked you to be involved in this."

"Tell me, what will you tell your brother?" I will tell him, I over heard them talking about how he is doing a bum job and that one of them could do his job better, so I acted first."

"You and Junior need to excuse yourself from the party and meet me in my room.

I have something to say about tonight and it can't wait."

I found Junior by the pool being himself, a spoiled brat. "Uncle wants to see us." Let's not keep him, Cousin." "You cousin, Junior said, you are a ruthless mother fucker.

You know some people have a problem killing four men in one night, but I see you can stomach it.

I'm glad we are not enemies." I looked him in the eye, just before we opened the door to my uncle's room.

"We will never be enemies. I am your right hand and who can be without their right hand. No different than me shooting that guy in Adams Morgan. Together we can handle anything, understand?" "Yep, Primo, I do."

I had never been in my uncle's room. It was decorated like an old western saloon with pictures of horses and saloon paintings adorning the walls. "I want you two to look at the pictures on the walls. Each man you see is a cartel member and a friend of our family. These men died protecting me when I was the Domo.

Either the other families wanted to kill me or the government wanted my head. Whatever the fight was, these men were there to die. You, Junior, will one day be the Domo. DaVaughn, your father could never understand how we live here, but your Grandmother, who is my sister, comes from the same life.

Junior, your father is the Domo, Yes, but the Kidd family has supported us with lots of money. Your father is a better Domo than me, I will agree, but you will be better than him.

You two, protect each other. Now, that you have shed blood once again together, both of you give me your finger and I will make it official between you two. Each will be responsible for the other.

I, being a senior member of this family have the power to do this. I know both of you and your fathers and they would want this marriage of our families again reunited. Do you to agree to die before the other is killed?" We nodded Yes. "And DaVaughn, do you accept Marcel as your Domo?" "Yes sir."

"With this pin, I prick your hands and with this saint, we merge your bloods. You two have made me proud, so now go back to your party and I am glad to see that if it has to be done, we have two killers to protect this family. Kissing his hand, we both left his room feeling like we had just been given the keys to the city.

"We didn't have time with all the commotion going on today to give you your surprise. So, I'll tell you. I smuggled all your money you left in the states back to you here." "Are you telling me that you have saved me again?" "Yep, it seems that's the way for us. Let's get back to the party now. We have a lot to celebrate.

Months later, a plan in motion is what it was to celebrate! I was back in America and we all had our orders. We received the weapons and the cash as promised. Cliff called me a few months later at the cabin and told me that we were winning.

"I need for the rest of those names to become history. Get the word out that it's time to finish this thing once and for all. You need to make a trip home and I will meet you guys there." I was happy. I was home sick for Mexico anyway. I hung up the phone after we talked and began leaving messages for the gang.

The only thing I would say to each of them is you have a telegram. They all knew that, that meant we needed to meet in Mexico City. I called the airport to see what they had available. I wanted to leave from Dulles Airport and to my surprise, I got a first-class flight for regular class. That was even better, considering how long the flight was.

I packed my bags light because I had clothes at Marcels'. It took me a couple hours to lock down the cabin. I didn't have a good car. I just had my pickup truck and I headed to Washington to let my dad know I would be leaving. I wanted to see him. It had been some time since we saw each other.

I got to the house late in the evening and I was glad that he was there. I didn't want to leave without seeing him. I walked in the great room where he was reading over some papers. "So, my little boy has come to see me. I hope with news that you are doing good and that you are on your way home."

"It's funny you should say that. I have a flight out in about three hours." "Are you Ok, my boy? Come, sit close to me so I can see you." He lifted my chin from my chest and said, "You have no need to fear me. I am here for you and it is Ok.

We all make mistakes. Go check on my mother for me and we will chalk this all up as a bad experience. Did you know that Junior is in the hospital? They say it is his heart. I don't know, so make sure you go see him.

I asked your Grandmother if it was serious, but she didn't say much. I will level with you. I don't think it's his heart, you get my drift? I have some people coming here in a minute and I don't want them to see me emotional, so let's get our good byes out now."

He grabbed me and kissed me on both cheeks. "You, my son, make me worry so, but I could not have asked for a better son to love." Then he hugged me. "Go and make sure my mother has everything she needs and if there is anything, just let me know.

She has the new house and I fear it may be too much for her, so try not to spend all your time at Marcels'." I wanted to tell him so bad; I'm in a fight with Cliff and I fear for him, but when he asked about Cliff, I just told him that he was just traveling, so he can find out what he wanted to do with his life.

The real reason was that he was being hunted as he was hunting. My father reached in the side of his desk and opened an envelope and gave me a few thousand.

"I know you don't need it, but what else can a father do, but help. Do what you know is right, my son. I can see you are not telling me something and that detective has been calling me. I'm glad you are going to Mexico. I hate being involved in this type of thing.

Have you been keeping up with your stock I told you about? It's way up. You should be sitting on a nice little nest egg. Don't let it get you in trouble. I think we should make the cabin your permanent address. It will be my birthday present to you. You can have the furniture too."

"Thanks, dad! I love it up there. Mountain life is great for me."

"Ok, my son. It's almost time for my appointment. Tell Marcel Senior that I will send him some money and that I have something for him. He'll know what you mean." We walked to the door.

"What is that thing in my drive way?"

"It's my car. I didn't want to attract any attention in West Virginia." "Good thinking. I will have someone take it back for you. Go call a limo.

You might as well go in style, so that way you can just relax on the way to the airport. Just tell the driver to charge it to my account. Now scoot, I have work to do.

I arrived in Mexico early in the evening. I called the ranch and asked if they would send someone to pick me up from the airport. I told them I would be waiting on the south side of the claims department and to put me through to Junior's line.

"Hello." "Hey, you shit! It's me, DaVaughn, and guess what, I'm here in Mexico City."

"You are? I'll have someone pick you up." "I already asked Madeo." "Ok. Well, I'll send some men with him. It's pretty rough, now that we are at war.

I have missed you so much. I could use your quick thinking. My padre is driving me crazy. I can't come to the airport, sorry. I am only allowed to go into town and back."

"That's Ok, Junior, I have to go see my Grandmother, then I will be to see you. Can't wait to see you brother." "Me either. We will throw you a party and invite all the girls from town. It's going to be big, so get ready to be the man of the hour. We will announce it to the public that you are a member of the Delprado Cartel.

I got to my Grandmother's house and as usual she was sitting in the kitchen listening to old mariachi music. I crept in the door and yelled, "Who loves their mother more than anything in the world?" She leapt up from her seat and ran and gave me a hug and kiss. I felt so happy to be home and I could tell she missed me. It is so good to have you home she said. I have missed you so.

Go take your things to your room and I will make you some real Spanish food just the way you like it." "I gave her a hug and I went to my room. The phone rang and I heard her answer it. "Yes, he's here. I'll go get him." That was all I could make out. "Mi amore, the telephone is for you. It is the Domo." "Hello, Senior."

"You are to come see me, the Domo, whenever you come in town. Don't let this happen again. Come here to the rancho now.

I want to talk to you before your American friends come." Hearing
the seriousness in his voice, I answered very respectfully. "Yes, my
Patron, I am on my way now." "I'll send Madeo back for you and
you don't leave the rancho until I have spoken to you.

Tell your Grandmother I summoned you. I will be going to
Chile, so I won't see you till tomorrow sometime, but you are to
stay here when you are in town and go and spend time with your
Grandmother. I know how much she missed you. Be careful, do
not take Junior out of our town, understood?" "Yes, Patron."

Then he hung up the phone. I will have to go to the rancho
Mama, so don't wait up for me." "Oh good, it's good you are going
there. They love you so much. Junior talks about you all the time.
Now come get something quick to eat and wait for the car down
stairs, you mustn't keep Marcel waiting.

The car dropped me off at dusk time. It was very chilly out. I
asked why I had to walk up and the driver just said, "bomb" and I
got the drift. I walked up the drive way slowly.

My bag was so heavy from all the money I stashed in it. Then
from nowhere, I heard screaming, "Who are you? what do you
want here? Put up your hands." I think back and I use to not be
able to understand but very little Spanish, but how funny the brain
works to comply when you are scared shitless.

"Senior it's me, DaVaughn." "Oh, I'm so sorry. It's just that
the house is under strict orders." He ran and grabbed my bag and
shook my hand. "Good to see you again. Again, I apologize for the
gun. It is understood that you are a member now. You can count
on us anytime. I will put your bag in the lobby of the main house,
my friend." When we got in eye sight of the house, I saw Junior
on the porch. "Is that you, my cousin?

"We shook hands first, then we both looked and said the same thing at the same time, "I missed you cousin." "So how have you been cousin?" "Good." "And you will feel good too, tomorrow. Just trust me that tomorrow, that face will chuckle for joy. "Come on, cousin, just a hint. I will get no sleep tonight if I don't know."

"That's the point. My father tells me that you and your brother are at war. Too funny how our families live the same life, isn't it? But if l know your brother, cousin, it's very bloody for you guys." "Bloody is an understatement. I'm here to ask for help. That's why I'm here." "I don't understand," Junior replied.

"We can't speak on the phone in the United States or be seen together, so we have to meet here in Mexico to talk things out. This helps with keeping the Feds out of our business." "That's smart cousin. My father should use that method. Pretty damn smart! I'll tell my father of this. He'll think I'm learning something. Already, you are helping me DaVaughn."

"Junior, do you think your grandfather would talk to me about a problem I have?" "Sure, he's where he always is in the kitchen chomping on a cigar." "Do I have permission to talk with him you think?" "Oh yea, Junior said, my father tells him everything." "Don't take this the wrong way, but I need to speak to him alone.

I'll catch up to you later." "Ok, I will be in one of the barns. They have a copper head and a black snake. It should be a good fight. Oh yeah, you should be very respectful with him, he is easily offended." "Thanks, I will remember it.

The kitchen smelled like fresh, roasted peppers. It was very big and in the corner was a table that sat under this Spanish Mosaic that shined from the fire place. "Excuse me Senior, It's me, DaVaughn."

"Oh, come in my son, sit down, and talk with me about the

Americans." "I would like to speak with you Sir, I mean Senior."
"Please, my son, he said, think of me as your own father. Tell me
what troubles you? Speak freely to me, my boy."

"I need two pistolerdos at my bidding while I'm here. I want
them to have American visas, so I can take them back with me. I
am asking for guards." "Oh, no problem. How old do you want
them to be?" I decided to pick the young guns.

"You may borrow two ranch hands for ten thousand a piece,
U.S. dollars. Agreed? I will let my son know of your request, but
you will still have to ask for his permission. Remember this, the
head of the family has control of all men, even their fathers. You
mention it to him first, then I will come plead your case. He is due
back late tonight.

Now I have to ask you, my son. Are you in any danger?" "Aren't
we all, because of what we do?" "You are so much your father's
son. He is so quick with the tongue, a real thinker. Give my grandson guidance.

He is turning into a bandit. He robs and steals because of his
family's name. He is supposed to set the example for the others and
I'm afraid his father is not beyond making an example out of him,
you get what I am saying?

Who is going to respect a man who is not respectable? Junior
is smart, but he chooses not to use it at times. He has the killer
instinct, but does he have the family leader quality? I want you to
keep me posted on his development and I will pave your way with
the Domo." "Since we are on the subject, Uncle, I need to stage a
little coup d'etat.

My brother has enemies in our little thing. One of my cousins
is too greedy for my taste and he is a real killer, so I want to strike

first before he tries for my brothers place." "Oh, I see, but this, I cannot help you with.

But cheer up my boy, I know who will. The Domo is fond of you and he told me great things about your brother; so, I don't see why he should not help you, for a fee, of course. He was so pleased with how you got Junior out of that incident.

Whatever happened with that any way?" "Junior was disrespected first and things just got bad fast." "Junior tells me that you risked your life for him. You do know that when it is his turn, he will send for you?

He says, he going to surprise you and make you his counselor. That's a big honor. He says that if you were Spanish, you would be a Domo with no question. He is a thinker. Junior sees this family in the trafficking business, but he wants to get more into the storage end instead of the real trafficking. So, you see, he is thinking and we both chuckled.

One day, when you have time, my son, will you explain the world of stocks and bonds? Junior tried, but he didn't really understand it himself, but he says he will make us all millionaires with it. When he came home, he started telling us how the American markets work. He picks things up and that's good. You just remember, if you protect this family's future, it's like, writing your own."

Chapter 13

LIVE BY THE CODE, DIE BY THE CODE

As I reflect, on how this whole deal was going sour for me, I have to say, the first moment was meeting with Don Marcel after his trip to Chile. He wanted me to help him get into the States more. He wanted to have more access to the Black ghettos.

He offered to help me kill my brothers crew, if I agreed to convince my brother that the two men that were representing the Delprados interest, should be allowed to have their own ghetto street to blow out with the coca and Cliff could just be a collector.

Sounded good then, but what I didn't know was that he planned on moving Cliff out the way the whole time. It just so happened that I unknowingly offered him the golden apple. You see, if he killed the crew, it would make it that much easier to remove Cliff, so I am just to blame for this mess I'm in.

Cliff called. "I have been trying to reach you guys. How is everything going? Are they being respectful to Don Marcel?" I didn't say anything, I was at a loss for words. Then I blurted out, "I killed them all. I overheard them bad mouthing you and saying things like, if we can find a connection while we are here, then why go back to working for another mother fucker, family or not?

I panicked and I set the wheels in motion and that was that." "Are you fucking crazy, DaVaughn? "They were family, you idiot! I needed them to fight for me.

Now, I'm here alone like a sitting duck. How dare those fucking Delprados make a decision like this and not check with me! I am the boss of that crew and they have insulted me more than ever. What the hell, DaVaughn? I thought you loved me.

You have just sentenced your brother to death. I have two targets left on this list and I'm under indictment, so they are watching me. The Feds are so far up my ass, I had to move out the hood.

I say how it has to be, not them. You make whatever excuse you need to, but you get your ass back to the states, Now! I am under attack on all sides and you kill my crew? I still don't know what you were thinking." "If I may speak, I was thinking that if, they all decided to kill you, you would be dead.

That's what I was thinking." "Damn, I will handle the last two targets myself. It seems to me, little brother, it may not be Antone or the rest I should have been worried about." He hung up the phone. All I could think was, you idiot, I am protecting you!

I got back to the states about two weeks after my blood spree. I went back to the cabin where I knew Cliff would have to come deal with me on my own turf. I got a call late one evening from him. "I'm here at the exit and you better have something good to tell me." Then the phone went dead. Thirty minutes later, I got the knock at the door. I stood up from my Dad's chair and walked and opened it.

"You idiot," he said, punching me furiously. You have cost me my dream. My crew is dead. My favorite cousins are dead. You will pay for this. I came to tell you that you are not my brother anymore. You are the enemy, as far as I am concerned. I will make you pay. The last targets have to go now before they become witnesses at my trial.

If they live to next week, you won't." Then he turned and walked out the door.

As he walked to the car, I could hear him shouting. "I hope they will protect you, because all deals are off. I'm not paying them shit. Tell the Domo I said "fuck you" from me and I will be taking the house, the money and the coca that is stashed in it.

Tell him that he knows I know. Oh yeah, you trader, you can also inform them that I have dealt with my so-called partners they sent me." "If you are saying what I think you are, I yelled, then we're both dead."

I ran back in the cabin to call Junior, but his father answered the phone. "I knew you would call. I'm trying not to lose my temper, so I will let you talk first, he said." "I'm sorry first, Domo, my brother thinks you want to double cross him and move him out the way. But that's crazy. He is losing his mind. I apologize for him.

Please spare him." "I cannot do that. It's not me, he offended. It's my father, that he has offended. One of those men was his Godson. He has asked for your brother's life for such an offense.

He feels double crossed that he helped you protect him and your brother kills his Godson. It has to be done.

I'm sorry. Junior has already pleaded for you and I told him the same. It now is a family matter and the family voted and that is that.

I hate to hurt your father, but I must now do my duty and make this right. You must now choose the family you belong too and that is this one. Think of your Grandmother. She would tell you the same. The family must come first. He has wronged a senior member.

Disrespect is not tolerable. I tell you what DaVaughn, you handle what you must for your brother. I will stall what has to be done, so you can prepare." "Thank you, Sir." I can still feel the tears running down my face and the one thing that made it even worse was I was the one who introduced Cliff to this family.

I could not stop crying. I wanted to warn Cliff, but I feared he would just do more to hurt the situation, plus I knew he wouldn't listen. When he was ready to talk, I knew he would call. Then, I felt a shift in my mind and anger fell upon me.

I would take out my frustrations on the last two targets. I would make them pay for all my problems. It was silly when you think of it, but when you are backed in a corner, you bite and you bite hard.

I hoped that this would smooth it over a little between Cliff and I. I planned it all out. I knew that the two targets loved to go clubbing, so I knew that that would be my best chance to achieve my goal.

It was on early on Sunday, when I got a suspicious knock at the door. I ran and grabbed my gun and took my position. I yelled, "Who is it?" No one answered, so I cocked my gun and yelled again. "It's me, Madeo, Junior sent me to watch over you and to help any way I could."

I walked to the door and peeked out the window. Sure enough, it was him, and he was alone. I unlatched the door and welcomed him in with the barrel of my AKA starring at him. "You will not need that. I am here to help you out of this mess. May I come in, because I have nowhere else to go? I lowered my barrel. "I'm sorry, Madeo, things are crazy for me right now." "I know, my friend, he said and patted me on the back. It's time to do what you must do to survive." "Madeo, I have a good plan, I just need one more piece to it and I will be ready. For now, we will prepare for any unforeseen problem."

I went upstairs to the loft to make a phone call that I had been dreading to make. I had to have a pretty girl to get close to my targets, but I only could think of one person to pull it off. Valarie was so pretty. I knew no man could resist her. My problem was, how was I going to get her to go along with something so dangerous?

I picked up the phone and dialed her number, hoping it was still in working order. It started ringing and with each ring, I felt so nervous. "Hello." "Hello Val, it's me, DaVaughn." "Hi, she said with such a happy voice, I am glad to hear from you. I've been thinking about you since we met and I am so happy you called.

How is the gang?" "Fine. Hey baby, I said, would you like to come spend some time with me in the mountains?" "I sure would and I would like for it to be now. I know I sound like a nut, but I have missed you so much and I don't want you to get away again.

I know it sounds crazy." "No, it sounds beautiful. I didn't think you were that interested in me." "I didn't want you to see that I fell in love with you the first time I had sex with you, DaVaughn."

"We'll do this, I'll send a car to pick you up at Shady Grove Metro Station. That way, my driver won't get stuck in traffic." "Shit, I would walk, if you asked me to, DaVaughn." "No, that's not needed," as we both chuckled. "I'll buy clothes out there and I'm on my way to the train, so I will see you in a few.

What car will I be looking for?" "It will be a pickup truck." "A pickup truck?" and she laughed.

"You are so crazy, but if that's what it is, Ok with me.

Tell him what I look like, so I won't walk by him." "I will, baby, I will tell him to look for a woman that will steal your breath away." "How kind, DaVaughn. I will be there," and she hung up the phone.

Val came out to the cabin, I think, because some guy was stalking her, but what did I care? She was here and I needed her. I heard her come in and say, "I'm here, baby, where are you, Sweetie?" "I'm on the deck, off the master bed room."

She came out on the deck. "Why are you out here?" "I have something on my mind and I do my best thinking here." "Is there something I can do to help?" "I hope so. I might as well get this over with. I need your help to kill two men." "Wow, you really throw it at a girl, don't you?

First time, I ever been greeted like that. Not very subtle, are you? I respect that you shoot from the hip. How dangerous are the men?" "Let's just say, if they live, I die." "Oh damn, that serious? I'm not saying I will help you, but if you tell me more of what I am to do, I may be able to answer you." "Sit here. I'll be right back. I bought some good weed and I think now is a good time to roll one." We moved into the bedroom and sat around the fire place. "This is nice. Is this your house?"

"Yeah, my dad gave it to me." "Nice Dad, she said. So, let's talk. "Well it's like this. I need you to befriend, should we say this guy, pointing to the picture. I'm going to hire a prostitute to really get them worked up. You will tell them you run an escort service. Trust me, they will believe it. I will have a limo and you will be dressed the part. I need for you to get them to this address.

It's a real rich building downtown with an underground parking lot. That's where I will be waiting. I know that one of these guys loves coke, so you will have enough to make him think you have a connect to it. I will be waiting in the parking lot. Make sure you drink a lot in the limo and just to make sure they are intoxicated, I want you to slip a pill in their drinks.

The pills are very small. Just have the other girl suck both of them at the same time, that way you will have time to slip them the pills." "Ok, sounds good, but I don't want to be around when it happens." "Don't worry. Madeo will be dressed like a janitor. He will get on the elevator with you and then he will ask for you to go through the side door.

That's when you make an excuse that you need to get something out the limo. By the time you two get to the limo, it should be done. Just make sure that you get them to that door way. When you leave, I want you to go to Dulles Airport and book the next available flight to Mexico. It doesn't matter where.

You just have to be on that side of the border. You got it?" "And where will you be?" I will be in the car waiting for Madeo. We are going to leave from BWI airport, so don't worry. Call this number when you get to Mexico. They will take you to my family's house." "Wait, DaVaughn, Mexico? Why there?" "That's where my protection is, so if you want to be protected from American laws, I suggest you get there and get there fast."

"Ok, I get the drift but, let's talk. What is in it for me?" "What do you want? Name your price. I'm sure we can come to some agreement." She looked puzzled. I could tell she was thinking about it hard. Then it came out. "I want to be Mrs., I don't even know your last name." "Kidd. I'm sorry, baby, my name is DaVaughn Kidd."

"Well, then I want to be Mrs. DaVaughn Kidd. That's my price and I want to be married as soon as we get to Mexico, not a day after. That's my price. I figure, if I can get life in jail, I should be able to get a life with you," and she smiled. I have to ask you, "Why do you want me?"

"I don't know, but it's partly your age and it's partly the way you just, I don't know how to describe it. You see the world in a beautiful way and you show love. That's where you differ from most men. That's a great quality. I feel like you will love me forever.

So, if this is the price for true love, then so be it, my love.

I love you that much, but know this, I may seem kind and I may seem loving and gentle, but if you cross me and not marry me, I will make it a point to find you and that bitch you would have and kill you both. Understood?" "Understood", I said, with a slight fear of paranoia.

What did I just agree to? But I knew there was no other person to do the job.

"How long do you think we will have to stay in Mexico? I want to prepare. I can put my apartment in storage and then I will be ass free as a bird. I will need some money." "No problem. I will give you ten thousand in the morning. I have to wait till daylight." "Why?" "Can't find the damn tree I hid my cash in, in the dark."

We just laughed and laughed.

"Now let's get serious. Can you trust Madeo?" "I can trust him to be what he is, a hired killer. He knows he can't fail or it will be him that will die."

"You say that so cold." "Sorry, but I live life truthfully."

"I know and that is why I love you. I will be ready in one week, so set it up." I kissed her on her cheek and pulled her close. Her hair smelled like strawberries, her breath smelled of apples and her perfume was amazing.

She was the perfect lady and now she was mine. Just that fast, I had a wife. We spent all week together talking of Greek poetry and going over the plan and what she would need to leave the country. On her last night with me, she told me that I am the only man that moved her and she will love me forever, if I allow her. I couldn't help but think what if these targets are professionals and they smell a rat?

Then she would be dead and again blood on my hands.

The night finally came and both targets were spotted together. It was routine. The same usual clubbing on a Friday night. I had my friend follow them all day. She was a cutie too. I told her if she ever spotted them, to just flirt and promise them a night they won't forget.

She followed them to the Utopia Club. It sat on Georgia Avenue and it was perfect for a hit. It had two major escape routes. I could take 16th Street up to Route 495 or take Route 29 and head for Baltimore. Either way, each route could lead me to the airport. We parked across from the entrance, so we would see them come out.

We sat in the car that night, it seemed for ages. Then at around 2 am, I saw Valarie and Kisses, come out with the targets.

The limo pulled up and they all got in.

We followed them to the building and it was going like clockwork. I pulled out my gun and told Madeo that it was a change in plans. "What's changed?" "I'm going to kill them myself.

I have to do it." "No, my friend. I need you behind the wheel. I don't know the roads, so I wouldn't know which way was best for us to escape. I know you are concerned, but trust me, I will kill both men and the women if you want me too." "No, Valarie is my wife and the other is just a prostitute. Just keep focus on the men."

The car pulled in the parking lot and Madeo stopped at the corner. "I will walk from here. I will meet you on the other side of the building. We shook hands and he got out the car. I pulled the car on the other side of the building and

I waited. The clock said three o'clock. I would say twenty minutes went by, when I saw the limo go by, then Madeo came running to the car. He jumped in and said, "Go, go, go.

It's done, but I think I shot the prostitute. Well, I have to be honest. I know I shot her."

"Please tell me you didn't kill Valarie." "Oh no, man, I pushed the prostitute back in and I sprayed the elevator. I cut the buttons out the elevator. I saw your wife running to the car. She can really run man. She was running like a rabbit. You had to see it." "Are you sure they are all dead, Madeo?" "I'm sure.

I shot them all in the heart and the head, to be sure. Trust me, whoever has to clean that up, will hate his job." I stepped on the gas and headed for the highway. We got to BWI Airport and booked two flights that would leave at seven o'clock. Four hours to bum.

I was happy the plan was working out for me, but I wanted to know how Val was doing. Madeo came and sat next to me. "It went well, cheer up." "Yes, it went well, I said, but it won't help my brother. He is still going to die." "I know it.

The Delprados are not to be taken lightly, you know?" My father is one of the guys your Uncle showed you on his wall.

Take my advice, DaVaughn, when you get back, beg for your

brother's life." "I don't know what to tell my father." "If I was you, my friend, tell him nothing. You don't want him involved in this" "You are right. I will leave him out of it." "I'm curious though, what will you say to your Uncle?" "I don't know. I guess I'll just beg for his life and offer all the money I have and pray they accept it."

Time went by fast, because it was now time to board the plane. It didn't seem like we were there that long. I boarded the plane and I sat near the window, so I would not be disturbed. I bought some sleeping pills with me.

I took three and it was nighty night. I awoke to the sound of the captain telling the passengers that we will be landing in twenty minutes.

We landed and took a cab to my Grandmother's house.

"Hey, my love," I said, as I entered the door. Hello, my love," she said, as if to say, I know what is going on. "I came to see you before I go to the ranch. I have to stay there now." "I understand.

I will come visit you there and I will bring you those nice rolls you love so much. She gave me a hug and a kiss and said, "The man who lives with the gun in his hand and lives by the code, must also die by it.

Remember, that is the way." I called the ranch after we sat and talked for a while. Junior answered. "I'm here, Junior, at my Grandmother's." "I will send a car for you, Cousin. I'm sorry for your brother. I love him too. Remember that." Then he hung up the phone.

On my way to the ranch, I could have never been sadder. For once in my life, I have to really live the life I have chosen. I would rather be in shoot outs every day than have to hand my brother over. I can't think of anything I can do without putting my father in danger and we call ourselves family. We pulled up in front and I'm not seeing things clearly.

My head feels like someone let a bomb off in it. I have walked this drive way so many times, but this time, I felt like I did when I was in the boys' jail. I didn't want to be here, was all I could think. The flood lights came on and I was blinded for a minute. "We were told to search you and your bags." "So, I will take this for you and please go to the main entrance.

My cousin says, you have a great cabin and that we all could live on the land you have. It must be a lot because it's fifty of us. I think Junior is waiting for you so you shouldn't keep him waiting." I rang the doorbell several times, when I got to the door. It seems like I was made to wait.

The guard finally opened the door. "Hello, Sir, please take no disrespect, but I was told that you must change your clothes and that you are to have someone with you at all times.

Please change and then I will take you to the Patron." I changed and then was led to the study. "Stay here, I will announce you." He entered the room and then I heard a stern voice yell, "Get in here right now." I was trembling, but I couldn't stop my fate, that was on the other side of that door.

"Do you know why I am upset with you?" "Yes Sir," I answered. It's because of my brother." "How can I kill Michael's son after he saved mine?

Did you tell your father about this matter?" "No, I didn't want him to get involved." "Thank you, thank you. I would hate to have to deal with that too. Now you see what it is to be the Domo.

Not what you thought, is it? He is a murderer of his own family. You have to have your own family's blood on your hand. Do you see how a man can make the decision to murder his own family? Forgive me for my yelling, but I hate this. I really liked your brother and my son loved him.

DaVaughn, my father is from the old world. When your brother killed his Godson, he crossed a line that no old schooler would ever tolerate. I want you to know that you nor your father are in any danger. It is between this family and your brother. Junior has tried to plead for you. He even shed tears. He told me about your pact. He feels so bad as I do, but your brother drew blood first.

Whenever Junior would talk to my father, he would dismiss him. This is the job, you will one day have to do, something you hate, but know it has to be done. So now I ask you. How can I trust that you will not one day seek revenge for your brother?

You are smart. You are a man now and I have to think of you as such. I will tell you this. In return for your loyalty, I will give you twelve kilos and you will be allowed to have all the money your brother stole from me.

On one condition, you will return to Junior and will resume your duties to him when it is his time. Now, go get yourself together and find strength within yourself to get through this." "Yes, I will find strength in myself and I want you to know that Cliff loved you. He dreamed of being a man like you." "I'm so sorry, my son. Take this kiss on the cheek and know my heart is as heavy as yours is."

I got up and walked out the door towards Junior's room with my guard at my side. Junior came out of his door and told the guard to go away. "I am so sorry, my brother. I am in so much pain and it hurts me too see you like this.

I will one day make it up to you. I swear. I thought to myself, my brother will not die in vain. I am a member of one of the meanest cartels and I will make this industry pay one day.

Trust me. It will bow to me and I will use it to do my bidding. "Are you Ok, brother? You seem somewhere else." "No, I was just thinking that nothing will separate us. I need you now, more than ever, Junior. This must never happen again in our families.

From now on the American side of this will run with the same discipline as in Mexico." "So, I hear you have a wife now?

She called here and she made sure I knew that she was Mrs. Kidd." "I didn't know the outcome of this, but I have to be honest.

They could have said, you too must die, so I didn't want to involve her. "She is in an apartment on the upper side of town. My grandfather put her in the best place. If you would like, I could have someone go get her.

She has been calling here every hour." "I'll get her. I have to marry her here in Mexico. Do you know a church I can go to?" "How about this? I will pay for everything. I will set it up and I will have so many flowers for her. It's the least I can do." "You do that, Junior you do that."

Three weeks later on a hot ninety-five-degree day, Val and I was sitting in our room at my Grandmothers, just talking about the ceremony Junior threw us. It was a scene out of the movies. So many people!

We were married in a small town. The church was the focal point of the town, so when someone gets married, the whole town shows up.

Val looked so beautiful, like a Spanish princess. "So, Mrs. Kidd, what are you thinking?" "Well Mr. Kidd, she said, I am just looking at this ring and I am so happy and giddy. Thank you, baby, for keeping your word. I have to tell you the truth, baby.

I thought for a minute when I was sitting in that apartment that you were going to have them kill me. No baby," I said, I will never have such a thought when it comes to us baby, never."

I heard the phone ring, then I heard my Grandmother scream, "Oh no, Heavens, no." Then she yelled for me. I knew what she was going to tell me. "It's your father." I picked up the phone with a shaking hand. "Hello, father. What's the problem?" "My son, my son, your brother was killed this evening in an ambush shooting. He and two others were killed in his car by two other people riding in the car.

Please come home. I need to see you son." "I am so sorry, dad. I know how hurt you must be. I'm on my way home. I love you." Then, I hung up the phone. "You will have to go home?"

"Yes, grandmother."

"I cannot travel. My heart is too weak. Oh, my boy, she said, as she wiped the tears from my face, I know how you loved him." Val came down the hall. "What's wrong?" "My brother was killed today."

"I'm so sorry, baby. Let's go talk it through." "I want you to bring a lock of his hair," Grandmother said. "I will do just that, Grandmother. I will go see Don Marcel. He will help us. We will be leaving out as soon as I can find a flight out."

I went to my bedroom and prayed. They say major things in your life can change you and losing my brother did. My family killed my brother. How is that possible for me to swallow? I never got to talk to him since our big argument. What a horrible way to leave things between us.

We arrived the following day in the states, Val and me. My father picked us up. My father looked so bad. He looked as if he had been crying on the way to the airport. "I can't believe he's dead," he said. I knew he was no saint, but who would want to kill him. It looks like an inside job.

One of his so-called friends, I suspect. I want to tell you something and he leaned in and said, I don't know why I feel like this, but this wreaks of a Delprado. I feel it in my gut." "I don't think that dad. They loved him." Then it happened, a tear ran down my face. They loved him. Right. When we got to the car my father said, "I am in no shape to handle this, so I want you to bury your brother.

Your mother blames me. She said I should have not given him so much money. I use to tell her, it's his money, not mine but she would never listen. You are going to live back in the cabin. I don't want you in the city. I know you, my son. I want you to stay in the states now. Do not try to find out who killed him. Do you understand? You stay out of it, my son.

I could not stand to lose you both. You do know that your brother named you as his beneficiary on his life insurance policy? He had two policies. One was worth two hundred and fifty thousand and the other was for one hundred and seventy-five."

I could see it was killing my dad to tell me all this information. "And you are to take control of all his stock options. The lawyer will go over all this with you soon." "I don't care about that stuff, Pop.

I'd trade it all for Cliff to come back." "I also have something else for you, son. It is his watch. I know he would want you to have it." I grabbed my dad's hand and I tried to affirm to him that I am here for him.

We pulled up in front of Cliff's apartment. "So, this is where he was living? Pretty rich, if you ask me. Val and I will go up alone. Go get something to eat around here and we will meet you back here in an hour." "You will have to pack his things up or hire someone to do it." "Don't worry, I will handle it."

"Oh yeah, my son, here are the keys to the cars he had. Those are yours too." I went in the building and walked toward the elevator.

The key ring had a tag on it that had A-12 to A-16. That would explain the key ring. He would always say, "I have one hundred thousand on this key ring." I got to A-12. There was a car with a cover on it.

I pulled the cover off and what did I find; a 300 CE Benz. A-13 had a 91 Porche, A-14 M class BMW,

A-15 Honda fast bike and A-16 a 928 Porche, like in the movie Scarface. I found thirty kilos and two hundred and fifty thousand in cash in his safe.

I broke down crying again. It wasn't worth the price. A note I read in his safe said, "If you are the Feds, fuck you. If you are a friend, fuck you and if you are in my crew then we all are fucked."

I went to his bedroom and lifted his mattress, because I knew that's where he would keep his gun and I had to have it. I found six hand guns and a quarter stick of dynamite. I also found some herb in his dresser drawer and I rolled a blunt and got so high. I woke up to the phone ringing. It was my father. "I'm sending some people to help you."

I decided to take the things I wanted to remember him by. I packed a few shirts, hats, and a couple of jackets. I took his favorite hat that he had which was autographed by Michael Jordan. He loved that hat. I gave the house a last once over.

I got to the door with my bags and I just stared at the man that was no more. Then I shut the door and I called some friends to help me drive the cars to the cabin.

I took the BMW because I knew he loved those cars. I picked up Valarie and we headed for the mountains. On my way there, I kept saying that not just one man will die with you, many will go with you, brother. You shall rest your feet on their heads.

Chapter 14
THE CONCLUSION AND HEART OF THE MATTER!

I am asked all the time, was the street life easier and my response is always the same, No, but I know my people can identify with it when I try to describe finance. I was asked to write a plan for my people to follow, so they may achieve economic freedom.

I thought hard and long on how I could put it in the lamest terms, no double talking, just simple formulas. Wall Street is not as complicated as it looks, so I'll approach the subject from this angle. Yes, you are a big part of the wheel of Wall Street. Each time you buy anything, you are turning the wheel of the markets.

For example, babies are born every day and diapers used continually, yet my people have yet to connect that diapers are a product that you can feel safe investing in or creating a company that manufactures diapers for our people. Diapers are used in such a high volume by our people that it would do well in the baby market. To truly obtain economic freedom, you must see everyday products as startup businesses.

We must train our people to get out of the habits of buying products not manufactured by us, by doing so, we will create companies that will buy up the leading competitors. We need to retrain our minds to understand that if I buy it and my neighbors and families buy the product, then I must find this product in a minority company. I also think that if you can't find the product, then you must train your mind to realize that if you recouped all the taxes you pay out in goods, you will be on the road to creating a surplus of cash for future investing.

I like the diaper example, because we all can identify with it. Diaper companies will forever be in demand. Let's think how many products you have in your house that is disposable. I will take you through your house.

Kitchen equals dish cloths, brushes, sponges and hand sanitizers.

Bathroom equals tissue paper, cleaning detergent, tooth brushes and tooth paste, body and hair products.

I want you to now use this as your beginning for each of the following above products in your house, Write down the name of the product and the manufacturing company. These companies will start your portfolio. Investing is like street hustling, buy low, sell high or as we know the formula on the street buy low, hold the product until the street dictates that there is a saturated market driving the product down so you can buy and sell it for a higher price than the original purchase.

Our people have been taught to buy products, but not buy stock.

America is built on commerce and leveraging money. I teach my crew using this example, you make ten dollars per pay period, yes, something so small can be used to gain a position in the market.

I tell them, find me two stocks that I can invest $2.50. Invest the ten dollars until you obtain one hundred shares, this will insure portfolio growth. I teach that you don't need large amounts to build a portfolio, what it takes is discipline and allocation of funds.

I buy cars the following way, I invest in the automobile company and the bank I plan on using to obtain the loan for the car. I also invest in the automotive sector. I invest until I have enough dividend check coming in to pay half the car note. Use this method for every purchase and you will see your portfolio grow,

I am amazed that people don't invest first to create revenue to help pay for assets purchased. I ask the question. Do you have a car? I am most often told, Yes.

Then why don't you invest in the energy sector or in oil? To truly be a great investor, you have to step back and look at your everyday consumer purchases, then follow them back to manufacturing corporations.

I'll go further into this by giving this example. You're thinking of buying a house. I look at the bank I'm going to use to finance the house. I invest in the bank that offers shareholders lower rates on money borrowed or the give interest free time on the loan.

My chief focus is finding a bank that will give me a quarterly dividend check that I can use to double up on payments, this helps you pay more toward principle loan. In every publicly traded company, you will find revenue statement earning reports and by laws for shareholders. The most important fact I want you to gain from this example is that you can get help from the different sectors you invest in to help pay your outstanding debts.

I hope I have your attention because I think I have given you a great foundation for the next investing tip. I once asked GOD for a talent and I was told by Him to read the bible. I answered, "GOD, I have read the bible, I read it every day. I don't think you are understanding me," I said, "I need a talent from you.

I was told again, read the bible," His voice was so clear, I knew it was Him. I said, "Ok, so I went back to

Genesis and began reading it again, but I couldn't help but think, everyone reads the bible. A light switch being pushed up went off in my head, He said, Yes, most read my book, but most miss my blue print for success.

I want you to read my book, cover to cover this time. I want you to use your talent, then it was revealed. I was to list all commodities found in the book. I was given this example; a shekel is silver. I want you to use the list I gave to Moses to build the tabernacle, list the textiles and precious metals, the stones in the Priests' chest for the twelve tribes. These are mining companies. Pharaoh's chariots are tank manufacturers, which you will find in the defense sector.

The arrows of the bow men use are ballistic missile companies and ammo manufacturers.

The Cedar of Lebanon is lumber companies. The gifts given to Solomon from The Queen of Sheba, list them. The gold, the great quantity of spices and precious jewels are commodities.

The purpose of this, He said is to make it clear that there is a kingdom financial plan for my creation. The golden rule is be a lender not a borrower. Man reads it, but seldom applies it, GOD knows that if you put yourself in the hands of the banks, you will become a slave to them. Never use your credit limits unless you're going to buy assets.

Do you know that most things are marked up 100% over its

manufactured cost and sometimes more? In order to be free, you must grasp that your economic power is in being debt free. Man has corrupted the sheep, making them believe that having more at any cost is Ok, it's not Ok and it will cost you.

I want to now look at a sound financial plan, I use to get ahead and I want you to apply these following principles.

- Each pay period, you must buy a bond, stock and a precious metal coin.

- I want you to only use credit cards to buy assets stocks, bonds, and precious metals.

- Large purchases must be thought of the following way. Can I invest in the company first to qualify for a lower cost? Can I invest enough in the corporation to get dividend check to pay the note? Can I buy it used, to cut the cost of the purchase price?

Example
New car purchase
Invest in car companies that allow you to use the stock for part of purchase or where company shares qualify you for price consideration, because you are a shareholder.

Example
New home purchase
First look at the state bonds offered in the state the home is purchased. I want you to then look at banks you will be applying for loans from. Then invest in the bank that allows you to use shares to qualify for lower rates and see if dividend check checks can be

rolled into house payments. When the bond matures, you pay taxes up. Then buy another bond for future taxes.

Example

The following examples are for everyday life.

Food: Invest in grocery stores where you spend your money, this will allow you recoup the taxes back on money spent on food.

Oil companies: I advise my group to invest in oil companies that have credit cards, use the dividend check to pay card off or at least invest in companies to recoup taxes spent on gas purchases.

Electric companies which are in the energy sector, I invest in the power company I use for household energy or materials used by the power companies. Copper is used for electric cables. Find company that supplies the power company.

Retail clothing: I only invest in retail for taxes paid on purchases, so whatever companies you do your purchasing from, invest in it, so you can recoup the taxes back from purchases.

Cell phone: Buy stock, then collect dividend checks to pay bill up and buy newer phone.

Car insurance: Invest in the company or the parent company of the car insurance company to help with payments.

Health insurance: Invest in the provider or one of the Pharmaceutical companies who supply new and latest drugs.

When it comes to next generation planning, only give out bonds or silver coins, gold coins, stock, no cash and no depreciating goods.

I was taught not ask for anything, but to help my parents provide what I wanted. I would make a list of things I wanted from the grocery store, I then had to look at the bill, say a box of cereal and write down the company who manufactured the product. I then had to look in the paper and find the ticker symbol for the cereal company.

I was instructed by my father to write down the 52-week high and the 52-week low, then I had to track the stock. My father wanted my tracking report, if I had it, then I received the cereal I wanted. I know this seems like a lot for a box of cereal, but it gave me my investing foundation.

Presidents elected:

Each year a president is elected, my father taught me to invest in a defense sector on the third year of the previous president, so that you could profit from the new presidents' defense package.

It is now time to deal with how you must duplicate the following formulas in every market around the world markets that are strong and politically stable. The everyday quest must be to make a profit and leverage the profit out into future investments.

The greatest principle I hope you take from this is; You must take full inventory on where you are spending your money. I would like for you to write down every product you purchase. I want you to then start a house hold game of creating a list of stocks that you track. It is important to teach your spouse and kids.

My final nugget to you is this plan, I want you see your portfolio as a chair.

Leg 1 - Gold bullion or coin
Leg 2 - Silver bullion or coin
Leg 3 - Stock options
Leg 4 - 10% put aside of each check.

The seat is bonds that will mature to cover the down spirals of the markets for the following assets.

There is a reason why GOD has told us, be not of this world and do not look to the left or to the right, but look up. This world is built on financial slavery. The key to economic freedom is not listening to men of this world, but seek GOD

in your goals, in everything you do.

The world will drain you of your resources by trying to make you think you are accomplishing your goals by buying depreciating assets, in truth, by doing so, you are slipping a noose around your neck. GOD wants you to be free, He wants you to have nice things, but not if the very things you seek, enslave you.

I want you to turn off the television and start focusing on your economic freedom.

Dear children, brothers and sisters in CHRIST, go back into your bibles, turn back to GOD, seek him and all good things will be added to you. You can be free when you give back the chains of the one percent. There is a way to have your hearts desires, but GOD wants you to use common sense in obtaining them.

Made in USA - North Chelmsford, MA
1319287_9781794570092
06.23.2022 1341